Happiness is Homemade, Y'all!

Heartwarming stories and tried-and-true recipes
that celebrate the culinary heritage of the Deep South.
These cherished family recipes have
nourished our people, stood the test of time,
and been handed down through the
generations in Sweet Home Alabama.

Danna Standridge

About the front cover

Danna Standridge in her kitchen

About the back cover

Sydney Standridge enjoying time in her grandmother's kitchen.

Photos by Jackie Murray Photography

ISBN 978-1-7349622-0-8

Dedication

This book is dedicated to:

David Standridge, who puts the sparkle in my eyes

My family, for the deeply rich heritage you have imparted to me, along with your treasured tried-and-true recipes

My children and grandchildren, you are treasures from God above

Here's to all our happy and delicious times together.

Love y'all!

Danna

Also by Danna Standridge:

Time to Eat, Y'all! Celebrating the Culinary Heritage of Sweet Home Alabama

www.dannastandridge.com
Find Danna Standridge on YouTube and Facebook

Acknowledgments

A special thank you to Jimmy Parker for sharing his father's mementos from World War II.

Special appreciation to Jackie Murray Photography for the magical photos.

Some recipes were graciously contributed by Alabama cooks who generously shared their treasured family recipes. Complete listing index, page 143.

Foreword

Sweet Home Alabama, you hold my heart and my family roots going all the way back to the 1800s. When my ancestors sought a place to settle, I am so thankful that when they saw this land, they knew they had found their promised land. And I am so thankful they were smart enough to put down roots in the fledgling territory that would become the great state of Alabama.

Each and every family across Alabama has culinary traditions, family stories, and a deep heritage that has been handed down for many generations. These recipes have carried us through times of peace and times of war, through times of hardship and times of plenty, to nourish and sustain the people of this great state.

My first book, Time to Eat, Y'all, which celebrated the 200th birthday for the state of Alabama in 2019, went through two printings and was a limited addition. We are blessed to say it sold out quickly. The bicentennial book contains stories and recipes from my family.

Happiness is Homemade, Y'all! was published to meet the continued demand for these stories and recipes. This book contains new family stories and recipes along with those favored stories and recipes from Time to Eat, Y'all! I share them with you now from an abundance of joy and a happy heart.

Enjoy,

Danna

Table of Contents

One Alabama Family's Culinary Heritage and Adventures, Part 1 — 1

- You Learn a Lot of Important Stuff Eating at the Children's Table — 1
- Grandpa Campbell's Old Smoke House: from Digging Taters to Hog-Killin' — 5
- Home from the War, Part 1: God, Country, and Momma's Cooking — 9

Breads, Appetizers, Beverages, and This & That — 12

- Breads — 14
- Appetizers — 18
- Beverages — 21
- This and That — 22

One Alabama Family's Culinary Heritage and Adventures, Part 2 — 24

- Home from the War, Part 2: National Security, a Momma's Heart and Ugly Biscuits...God Bless America! — 25
- Nanny Swann's Famous Chicken-n-Dumplings: A Quest for Culinary Excellence — 28
- Oh Noooo...Not the Gravy! — 32

Salads and Soups — 34

- Salads — 36
- Soups — 31

One Alabama Family's Culinary Heritage and Adventures, Part 3 — 42

- Facing Tough Times with Southern Ingenuity — 43
- Granny Dera's Christmas Candy — Learning Our Culinary Lesson — 45
- Overthinking Football Can Get You in Hot Water — 47

Main Dishes 50

Chicken and Turkey 52

Beef 58

Pork 67

Venison 69

Fish and Seafood 71

One Alabama Family's Culinary Heritage and Adventures, Part 4 74

Poke Salat, a 15-pound Bible, and True Love 75

The Turnip Green Ministry 79

The Very Blessed Turnip Green Patch 81

Side Dishes and Vegetables 82

One Alabama Family's Culinary Heritage and Adventures, Part 5 94

The Marvelous Moma Holt 95

"With God as My Witness" ... 96

Southerners and Snow: A Delicious Phenomenon 101

Desserts 104

Cakes 106

Pies, Puddings, and Cobblers 117

Everything Else: Cookies, Candies, Muffins 126

One Alabama Family's Culinary Heritage and Adventures, Part 6 132

Passing It On with Grandma's Rolling Pin 133

Danna's Darlings and Family Favorites 135

What Did You Say? Understanding Our Southern Vernacular 139

About the Author 140

Index 141

One Alabama Family's Culinary Heritage and Adventures

Part 1

Pictured at the children's table is Jasper Standridge, grandson to the author.

You Learn a Lot of Important Stuff Eating at the Children's Table

I can remember playing outside after church on Sundays with my many cousins and hearing my Nanny come out on the porch and call us to the table, "Time to eat, y'all!"*

If you are one of the lucky ones who had the good fortune to grow up with lots of first cousins and Sunday dinners, then you had the treasured experience of learning all about your family and life in general at the happenings and goings-on at the Children's Table.

The many sets of twins at the Swann Sunday dinner. Danna is being held by her dad, Gerald Swann, who is second from the left on the back row. Dinah, her twin, is being held by Gerald's twin sister, Janet, who is third from left on back row. On either side of the group are Danna's great-grandmothers, Nancy Swann (left) and Mintie Thomas (right).

In large families across Alabama, it is every child's dream to one day graduate from the children's table at their grandmother's house. It's a place where you learn who you are and who your kin are as you dine on delicious food made by many aunts and grandmothers. Just so you know, I was still at the children's table when I was a senior in high school. We cousins just grew up together at that table.

For those of you with small families or those of you not blessed with knowledge or experience of this phenomenon, the children's table is where all little ones eat at their grandmother's house for Sunday dinners. It's the place where the grandchildren sit together and eat that amazing food that our aunts and grandmothers have cooked for the all-important Sunday dinners—which are actually at lunch time right after church—but we call it dinner to proclaim the importance of gathering to break bread as a family on God's holy day.

Now my most memorable children's table experiences happened at Popa and Nanny (Coy and Lorene) Swann's house. When I was born, I was named after my nanny, Danna Lorene Swann, and they lived right down the road from us. Popa and Dad farmed cattle together.

Nanny and Popa had been married a long time and had raised a large family by the time I came along. They held massive Sunday dinners at the little house they had built out of wood logged off their land back in the early 1900s.

You have got to understand how full that house was when we were all there. They had eight children and raised six children to adulthood. That's fourteen adults and eighteen children in their tiny home. (In quiet times while visiting with my Nanny as I was raising my own children, she would wonder out loud to me about the two children she had lost. Even though her house was always full with her large family at those Sunday Dinners, there were always two of them missing in her home and in her heart.)

Nanny and Popa Swann had twins, a little girl and a little boy, called Gerald and

* Southern vernacular, page 139

Janet. Gerald is my daddy, and he had twin girls named Danna and Dinah. I have three sets of first cousins who are twins and many in my extended family who are twins, so when we held get-togethers, we always had a picture of the whole group made, and then a picture of all the twins. Yes, our Swann family took the good Lord at His word when He said to go forth and multiply.

With six children, their spouses, their combined eighteen grandchildren, and the extra people who managed to drop in, the house was very full at Sunday dinners. The children's plates were helped* first, and then we were situated in the dining room and living room. The older children in their teens got to sit on the piano bench and the living room sofa and chairs. We younger ones had to sit at the dining room table with admonitions to be good and not to spill anything. (We tried to be good but inevitably someone usually did spill his or her tea after we got tickled about something, especially one of my younger cousins, who had a knack for it. My sisters and I realized this about him early on and always tried to beat him to the table so we wouldn't be right beside him and end up with his tea in our plate. Our younger brother, Tommy, usually got that spot, bless him.)

Popa and Nanny both came from very large families, and it wasn't unusual to have their brothers and sisters there. If any of our extended relatives came (and they did often

Nanny Swann with four of her six children

Nanny Swann's Best Roasted Turkey

As told to her granddaughter, Danna Swann Standridge

turkey
1 stick butter
salt

Thaw turkey in the refrigerator for approximately 2 days. When the giblets easily come out, it is time to cook.
Wash the turkey inside and out.
Butter and salt it, then wrap it in foil and put it in your roasting pan.
Bake at 325°, in general bake 20-25 minutes/lb. Check temperature in breast with a meat thermometer. Done at 165°.
Take the foil off for the last 30 minutes to ensure even browning.
You can tell it is done when the skin of the thigh is pricked with a fork and the juice runs clear or if the drumstick joint feels loose.

* Southern vernacular, page 139

for Nanny was known for her good cooking), Nanny would greet them at the door with the typical Southern lady's invite, "Did you eat yet?"* and then she would get them situated with a big heaping plate of food.

After everyone was served and before Nanny would put a single morsel of food in her mouth, she would make sure her whole clan was getting fed and fed well. Not one of her babies was allowed to be hungry on her watch. She would walk to every room and stand there quietly looking at every one of us and at our plate, and then she would say, "Do you have enough to eat?" After we assured her we did, she would go to the kitchen, sit in her chair, and help her plate. What an amazing woman my Nanny was! To this day, I am in awe of her ability to take such good care of so many people.

You know, you learn a lot of important stuff sitting at the children's table.

Nanny Swann's Chicken and Dressing

As told to Danna Swann Standridge

chicken, cooked and pulled apart into bite size. (Giblets are optional, but Nanny always used them. She chopped them and added them to the dressing but omitted the liver because of the strong flavor.)
2 cans of chicken broth, or broth used to poach chicken
2 pans cooked cornbread—let it sit out overnight to get stale
2 or 3 boiled eggs, chopped (optional)
2 eggs, beaten
sage, chopped, fresh (add a little at a time and taste the batter as you go till it is to your liking)
paprika

Crumble cornbread into large mixing bowl.
Roll sage between hands till it falls apart into bowl.
Add chicken.
Add hot broth one cup at a time till thin.
Stir in beaten eggs.
Gently stir in boiled eggs.
Pour into greased pan and sprinkle with paprika.
Cook at 350° till firm all over, about I hour.
Can freeze after cooking.

Lonnie Campbell's homestead for Hog Killin' Day in Hayden, Alabama, many years ago.

Grandpa Campbell's Old Smoke House and Granny's Fried Apple Pies

When I was a little girl, I loved going to my grandpa and granny's house. Lonnie and Opal Ilene Campbell did things in what was considered the old-fashioned way of the 1960s and '70s. (Now, in 2019 the funny thing is people are ***trying*** to go back to the way things were done then.)

You see, my Grandpa and Granny still lived farm-to-table just like their ancestors did before them. Their families had taught them to be self-sufficient just as they had done for many years. They grew a big family garden with everything from potatoes to peanuts to corn to tomatoes to okra. They had a cellar under their house to store the root vegetables and the other vegetables they spent all summer long canning. They even had a corn crib in the barn. (And if any of the barn cats had kittens, we learned their preferred location was in one particular corner of that corn crib. My sisters and I would crawl in there and cuddle those sweet little kittens.)

They even had a smoke house where they cured the meat they had raised on the farm. I remember as a small girl, I went in with Grandpa to salt some pork and stood up on my tiptoes to peek over the shelf where the pork rested. It was so dark in there that it took your eyes a little time to adjust. Meat was preserved on the shelves and hams hung from the rafters. And I just got to tell you, it smelled so good in that old smoke house. Years of smoke and meat aroma permeated that old shed, and it smelled heavenly in there!

And, I just loved it when it was time to get the potatoes in. Grandpa would get on the tractor and turn the ground so that the potatoes would be at or near the top of the soil. My two sisters and I would take off our shoes and go barefoot through the rows picking up potatoes. It was like hunting Easter eggs as we rifled through the dirt to uncover those cool dark potatoes that would eventually end up stored in the cellar to be enjoyed all through the year. But that Alabama dirt—it was so cool on our feet—I can still remember how happy that made me to walk barefoot through that dirt looking for potatoes.

Granny Campbell made the very best fried apple pies. If we got to her house and found apples drying in the sun, it was a heavenly sight. We grandchildren would play in the yard and sneak us a dried apple or two when she wasn't looking. They were very sweet and warm and leathery and chewy with lots of concentrated tart apple flavor.

As my mother tells it, my Granny would gather her apples as they ripened from her apple trees. When she had a basket or two, she would wash, peel, and thinly slice them. Grandpa had an old piece of tin laid on two sawhorses and placed it where it would get a whole day's sun. A clean cloth was spread across the tin and the apples were spread out on the cloth. The apples were placed in the sun daily until they were dried enough to store in a flour sack. Sometimes the flour sack would be placed in the sun until the moisture was all dried out of the apples. At days' end, my grandparents would take the apples inside. Sun-dried apples would be placed in gallon jugs for keeping to be used during the winter months.

Ilene and Lonnie Campbell, 1958

When Granny was going to fry up some apple pies, she would get about a double handful of the dried apples and put in a saucepan, and cover them over with about twice as much water as apples. She would get them to a boil, and then turn them to simmer until the apples absorbed the water and were soft. After adding sugar and a little cinnamon, the apples appeared dark and thick but not runny.

She would make her regular biscuit dough, roll it out thin, and use a saucer to cut the dough for the pie, place a tablespoon of apple filling on the crust, fold it over, and press the edges of the crust together with a fork. After all the pies were made, Granny used an iron skillet with enough lard to fry them in. After frying one side, she turned them and fried the other. It was always a treat when Granny made her fried apple pies!

And in the fall, when the weather was just right, excitement ran through the family when Grandpa finally decided (based on his calculations of the moon cycle, years of experience, and the cool temperature) that it was time to prepare the meat for winter. Yes, it was hog-killing time. At hog killing time, it was "all hands and relatives on deck." It was a serious amount of work by many hands to slaughter, prepare, and preserve the meat from the hogs that Grandpa and Granny Campbell raised on their farm. The succulent meat was divided amongst the workers as payment for the help, or the favor was returned and you helped them on their hog-killing day.

I remember walking into the kitchen during sausage making. Uncle Nelson was working the hand grinder, and there was a huge rounded-up heap of sausage piled on the kitchen table. Uncle Johnny, Granny, and Momma were adding seasonings to the sausage and kneading it in with their hands. And when Uncle Johnny pretended to taste a bite of the raw meat to check to see if the seasoning was right, I was both amazed and horrified and left the kitchen in a hurry so I wouldn't have to taste it next! But, I got to tell you, a little while later when the seasoning was just right, a batch of sausage was cooked up and we had some mighty fine eating.

As a child, I remember when I came to the realization that the pork chop I was eating was from that big hog that Grandpa carried me out to pet and feed scraps to. I had to get used to the idea. It took a little time, but I did.

Granny's Brown-Eyed Gravy

As told to Danna Standridge

white meat (salted side meat from hog)
water

Equipment:
skillet
drippings bowl

Go to smoke house and cut off a slice of white meat.
Wash off salt.
Fry meat in an iron skillet.
Remove meat when done.
While still hot, pour a cup of water into the grease.
It will boil and bubble, stir it down.
Pour into the gravy bowl.
Spoon gravy from the bottom of the bowl where the brown drippings are good and tasty. Spoon over biscuits, eggs, and grits.
The fat will rise to the top. Put a dollop of it in your beans and turnip greens for extra flavor.
Keep your drippings bowl covered on the stovetop.

Shirley's Fried Apple Pies

By Shirley Campbell Swann

Go to the Apple Farm and get a basket of apples. Wash, peel, and thinly slice. Place in a home dehydrator according to directions and dry apples. When dried, store in a covered container until use or store in a zip lock freezer bag in freezer.
When ready to make pies, add a couple handfuls of dried apples to pan, add enough water that is about double the amount of apples, bring to a boil then turn to simmer. Cover with lid. Cook till all water is absorbed, season with sugar and spices to your taste. Apples should be dark, thick, and not runny.
Make your favorite biscuit dough and place in refrigerator for an hour for ease of handling. Roll dough out as making biscuits. Use a biscuit cutter to cut. Now take the rolling pin and flatten into a circle. Add a tablespoon of apples, fold, and crimp with a fork. Fry in cooking oil in a deep fryer or pan. Turn over as needed to brown both sides. Place on a paper towel to cool.

Granny's daughter—my mother, Shirley—has adapted her mother's methods into a modern-day recipe for authentic fried apple pies.

Enjoy!

June 20, 1943
Dear Family
U.S. ARMY
1943
JUN 26
A.P.O. 698
Mr John n. Parker
Blount Springs
Route one
Ala.

Home from the War, Part 1:
God, Country, and Momma's Cooking

As America experienced growing pains and wars, so did Alabama. Our citizens stepped up to do their part to defend our country. We are savagely dedicated to our football, but more importantly, we are dedicated to defending our God and our country. During these painful times, mommas cooked and prayed, and our soldiers went off to war and dreamed of coming home to the love of family and Momma's home cooking. Many of my family members fought, bled, and some died in the different wars faced by America—World War I, World War II, the Korean War, Vietnam, the Gulf War, and the war in Afghanistan.

Great-Uncle Bert Swann was at Pearl Harbor when it was bombed, defended his country, then returned to Sweet Home Alabama to raise a family. Uncle Nelson Campbell was in Vietnam. Uncle Jack Daily was a sharp shooter in World War II and earned many medals. Among my many relatives who served was my Great-Uncle Loyd Parker. He fought in World War II and was in a prisoner of war camp for eighteen months. His family didn't know if he was dead or alive. They didn't hear anything to know his fate or his whereabouts.

Can you imagine the anguish the Parker family faced not knowing if he was dead or alive for a year and a half? The many tears and prayers that went up on Loyd's behalf? What got them through? A deep faith in God and many prayers and support from the community carried them through the wilderness of this tribulation.

Loyd's mother, Great-Grandma Parker, had her hands in the old wooden dough bowl making biscuits for the family when the joyous word came that he was alive and coming home. She wiped the flour off her hands with gusto and cried, "Whoopee! Loyd's coming home!" and left her biscuit making and ran down the road to tell her son, Avis, the great news, the answer to their many prayers.

When Loyd came home, a great celebration was held with lots of good hugs and his momma's home cooking as the whole community joined to celebrate.

I wasn't born at the time, but I'm sure one of Grandma Parker's yard chickens was on the menu.

Letter from Danna's great-uncle Loyd Parker to his family, World War II.

Yummy Chicken Pie

By Danna Standridge
In memory of Great-Grandma Maude Hardin Parker

3 lbs. cooked chicken, deboned
2 cups chicken broth, homemade or store bought
1 can cream of chicken soup
1 stick melted butter
1 cup self-rising flour
1 cup buttermilk*
pepper (to taste—I use 1 teaspoon)

Cut chicken into bite-sized pieces and spread into a greased 9"×13" pan.
Heat broth and soup till boiling and pour over chicken.
Mix melted butter, flour, pepper, and buttermilk and spread evenly over chicken.
Bake at 425° for 25-30 minutes or until browned on top.

*Hint: Don't have buttermilk? Use a cup of milk and add a tablespoon of vinegar. It will do the trick!

Opposite: Around the dining table at the Standridge home

Breads, Appetizers, Beverages and This & That

BREADS

Biscuits

2 cups flour, self-rising (we use White Lily)
1 cup buttermilk
4 tablespoons shortening, melted
melted butter for serving (optional)

Add flour to mixing bowl and form a well in the middle.
Add buttermilk and melted shortening in the well.
Stir till dough forms.
Pat with hands on floured surface.
Cut biscuits
Bake in preheated oven for 10 minutes or until light, flakey, and golden brown.
Options: top with butter, or melt butter in skillet and cook in butter.

Kim's Mexican Cornbread

cooking oil for skillet
1 1/2 cups self-rising cornmeal
1/2 cup self-rising flour
2 eggs
1 16 oz can of creamed corn
3–4 diced jalapeno peppers (I use jarred peppers to suit our taste)
pinch of salt and pepper
2 cups cheddar cheese, divided

Preheat large skillet with oil.
Combine next six ingredients and pour half into skillet.
Sprinkle 1 cup shredded cheddar over mixture.
Add remainder from bowl and top with 1 cup shredded cheddar. Do not put cheese close to the edges of the pan as it will burn.
Cook in a 400°-450° oven until done, about 35-45 minutes.

Poppy Seed Bread

Bread Ingredients:
3 cups Gold Medal all purpose flour
2 1/4 cups sugar
1 1/2 teaspoons baking powder
1 1/2 teaspoons salt
3 eggs
1 1/2 cups milk
1 1/2 cups Crisco oil
1 1/2 tablespoons poppy seeds
1 1/2 teaspoons butter flavoring, almond flavoring, and vanilla flavoring

Bread Directions:
Mix all of the above together with a mixer for 2 minutes.
Grease and flour 2 loaf pans.
Bake at 350° for one hour.

Glaze Ingredients:
1/4 cup orange juice
3/4 cup sugar
1/2 teaspoon of butter flavoring, almond flavoring, vanilla flavoring

Glaze Directions:
While still warm, combine the ingredients and pour over the top of the bread.

4 Generations Sour Dough Bread

Lorene Swann, Shirley Swann, Danna Swann Standridge, Lonna Dillard

"We can trace this delicious homemade bread through four generations in the Swann Family. It takes several days to make while working with the starter, the making of the dough, and the rising and baking of the bread, but it is surely worth it. A little butter and honey on a piece of sour dough bread hot from the oven is pure heaven."

1 cup bread starter (directions below)
1/2 cup sugar
1/2 cup corn oil
1 Tablespoon Salt
1 1/2 cup warm water
6 cups bread flour (be sure it is bread flour)

In a large bowl make a stiff batter of the above ingredients.
In another bowl that has been greased well with oil, put the lump of dough and turn over in the oil.
Cover lightly with plastic wrap and let rise overnight.
In the morning, punch down with your fist and divide into 3 parts.
Knead each part on a floured surface and put into 3 greased loaf pans and brush the tops with oil to keep from drying out.
Cover lightly with plastic wrap and let rise for 6 to 12 hours.
Bake at 350 degrees for 35 minutes.
Take out of the oven and brush the tops with butter.
Cool on rack, slice and enjoy.

Feeding your Sour Dough Starter

Starter is kept in the refrigerator except the day it is to be fed. The starter must be fed every 3 to 5 days to keep it active.

3/4 cup sugar
1 cup warm water
3 Tablespoons potato flakes

Take starter on hand out of the refrigerator.
Add above mixture and stir.
Let stand at room temperature all day, from 8-10 hours.
Take one cup out to make bread.
Return the balance to refrigerator.
Yeast is a living organism and must be allowed oxygen; therefore, make sure to have air flow in the lid of the container you use to keep your starter. I use a quart jar with a cover of foil with holes punched in it.

Sour Dough Starter

This is a one-time process to establish your starter.
If you know someone who makes the bread, get a cup of their starter and you will be on your way to wonderful homemade bread. Bread makers love to give the gift of bread making and will gladly share their starter with you. My Mom's starter is well-established as she has been making this bread for 35 years. I have been making it for the annual Thanksgiving feasts for David's family for over 20+ years and sent it to my children's teachers as treats at Christmas time.
If you do not know anyone with starter, make your own by mixing the following, covering it loosely, and allowing it to sit on the counter for 2 days until it smells fermented and starts to bubble.

1 package active dry yeast (2 ¼ teaspoons)
3 Tablespoons potato flakes
1/2 cup sugar
1 cup warm water

To feed your starter, follow the Feeding your Starter recipe to add to it and allow it to sit on the counter for up to 12 hours. Then, refrigerate for 5-7 days before making the bread. This process is only done the first time to get yours established.

APPETIZERS

Sausage Balls

1 lb. sausage
1 lb. sharp cheddar cheese
2 cups Bisquick
dash of pepper

Preheat oven to 350°.
Mix all ingredients and roll into bite-sized balls.
Bake for 15-20 minutes until golden brown and sausage is cooked.
Can be prepared ahead of time and frozen.
Thaw and bake right before serving.

Aunt Jan's Thanksgiving Celery

3 oz cream cheese, softened
3 tablespoons mayonnaise
1/2 cup pecans, finely chopped
1/4 teaspoon Worcestershire
1/4 teaspoon cayenne pepper
2 large stalks celery

String celery. Use only the most tender ribs. Cut into 3-inch lengths.
Combine remaining ingredients.
Spread the mixture on the hollow of the celery sticks.
Chill before serving.

Salted Pecans

1 lb. pecan halves
I cup heavy whipping cream
1/4 lb. butter
salt
Dash of cayenne pepper (optional)

Marinate pecan halves in cream overnight.
Preheat oven to 400°.
Drain thoroughly.
Place butter in baking pan and melt in oven.
Place pecans in melted butter.
Cook 5 minutes then turn pecans.
Bake an additional 5 minutes being careful not to burn.
Remove from oven, place pecans on paper towel to drain.
Lightly salt and serve. Can add cayenne pepper for spice if desired.

Jalapeno-Pimento Dip

"This is a fast and easy recipe that gets gone fast! Once you take a bite, you just can't stop eating it."

1/2 teaspoon garlic powder
4 oz pimentos
1/3-1/2 cup chopped jalapenos with juice to taste
1/2 cup mayonnaise
1/2 teaspoon dried mustard
8 oz sour cream
4 shakes of cayenne pepper (optional)

Mix all together.
Best if it is made the day before as it gets better with time.
Serve with assorted crackers.

Pimento Cheese

4 oz pimentos
1 cup mayonnaise
1/2 teaspoon onion powder
2 dashes garlic salt
4 cups shredded cheddar
8 oz cream cheese, softened
1 teaspoon cayenne pepper

Place all ingredients in the food processor and mix until well blended and the consistency is what you want.

Aunt Virgie Holt's Chili Sauce

1 gallon tomatoes
3 cups sugar
3 cups vinegar
2 cups chopped onions
4 pods hot pepper, cut fine
Salt to taste
1 tablespoon each: nutmeg, ginger, allspice, red pepper, black pepper, pickling spice

Peel tomatoes, chop fine, and add other ingredients.
Boil three hours.
Pour into scalded jars and seal.

Dinah's Stuffed Jalapeno Peppers

25 to 30 fresh jalapeno peppers, washed, cut lengthwise, and seeded, use gloves
1 package cream cheese
1 lb. sausage
1 to 2 cups shredded Parmesan cheese, per your tastes

Brown sausage and drain.
Mix in cream cheese and Parmesan.
Stuff your peppers.

Shirley Swann's Spiced Tea

14 oz Tang powdered drink mix
1/2 cup instant tea
1 envelope lemonade mix
1 3/4 cups sugar
1 teaspoon ground cloves
1 teaspoon cinnamon

Mix all ingredients together.
To make a cup of tea, use 2 heaping teaspoons of spiced tea mix for each cup and fill with boiling water.
Stir and enjoy!

Mocha Punch

1/4 cup sugar
4 tablespoons instant coffee
8 tablespoons chocolate syrup
3 cups boiling water
1 quart milk
1/2 gallon soft ice cream

Combine the first four ingredients together and stir till dissolved.
When ready to serve, add milk and ice cream.

Merry Christmas French Toast

1 loaf sour dough bread, sliced thickly
2 eggs
2 cups heavy cream
1/2 teaspoon cinnamon
butter for cooking

Have your buttered griddle or heavy skillet heating over medium heat on the stove top.
In a mixing bowl, combine eggs, heavy cream, and cinnamon.
Quickly dunk bread slice into egg mixture, and flip it so both sides are covered.
Pull bread out of mixture and let excess drip off.
Cook on both sides until they are browned.
Continue process until all bread is cooked.

Serve with maple syrup, homemade whipped cream, or fresh blueberry syrup.

Homemade Whipped Cream

1 cup heavy whipping cream
1 teaspoon vanilla
1 tablespoon confectioners sugar

In a mixing bowl, add heavy whipping cream and whip until soft gentle peaks form.
Beat in vanilla and confectioners sugar.
Do not overbeat or it will turn to butter.
Serve over desserts, pancakes, French toast, or fresh fruit.

Fresh Blueberry Syrup

1 cup fresh blueberries
1/2 cup water
1/2 cup sugar, can use more or less to your taste
1 teaspoon cornstarch
grated lemon peel, optional
juice from 1 lemon, optional

In a saucepan over medium heat, add all ingredients and stir well.
Bring to a slow simmer, stirring constantly until thickened.
Especially good over pancakes, French toasts, and ice cream.
Store in the refrigerator.

Frosty Homemade Ice Cream

1 can sweetened condensed milk
1 small cool whip
1/2 gallon chocolate milk
1/2 cup whipping cream (optional)
milk
ice cream maker
ice
ice cream salt

*Do not mix in a bowl.
Add the first four ingredients directly to the ice cream maker container. (It will not freeze correctly if you premix it.) You don't even have to stir it.
The mixer will do all the work for you.
Add enough milk to reach the fill line.
Follow your ice cream maker directions. Enjoy!

One Alabama Family's Culinary Heritage and Adventures

Part 2

HOME FROM THE WAR, PART 2:
National Security, a Momma's Heart, and Ugly Biscuits... God Bless America!

My own son, Caleb Standridge, graduated from the United States Air Force Academy, served in the Air Force, and defended our country in Afghanistan. I'm proud to say he represented his country, state, and family well and was decorated for his valor. We are proud of him and all our soldiers and their families who serve our country. When he was away from home for a time and in survival training maneuvers, with very little food rations, he told his fellow soldiers all about what he and my family call my "ugly biscuits."

Caleb Standridge, graduate of the United States Air Force Academy, 2007

How do I explain my ugly biscuits? You see, as is tradition in all good Southern families, my momma taught me to make biscuits just like her momma did and her momma before that. You know, the traditional way in which you mix the dough: roll it out on a floured surface, cut it with a biscuit cutter, and bake the dough that has been handed down for generations. They are lovely delicious biscuits and have been eaten and enjoyed in our family for many years. One day after getting home from work as a high school biology teacher, I knew my three kids and husband would expect my homemade biscuits to go along with the beef tips and gravy I had put in the crock pot that morning. However, I was bushed*, as we say in the South. I was so tired after teaching all day that I just didn't think I could do it. But we had to have something to sop up that delicious gravy. We Southerners just expect that.

What was I to do? One of my hobbies is reading recipes in vintage cookbooks. I thought of some recipes that I had read recently, concocted one right quick in my mind, and threw it together on a wing and a prayer. It was a cross between a drop biscuit, a scone recipe, and a topping for one of my chicken casseroles.

They smelled so good while they were cooking, and I was hoping for the best. When I pulled them out of the oven, they didn't look good at all. Those were the ugliest biscuits I had ever seen! They were a little flat and had all run together so that I had to cut them a part. I have to admit, those were the ugliest biscuits I had ever made in my whole life! Should I throw them out and start over with my traditional biscuit recipe? No way, I was too tired for that for sure. We were going to cover them with gravy anyway. Let's give it a go!

I put those ugly biscuits on the table hoping for the best. After they started eating, it got real quiet for a long time. I thought to myself, "Why are they not saying anything?"

Well, you can always tell when you got a good recipe because the family gets really, really quiet around the dinner table. My family was eating with gusto! So, we decided I should write down the recipe and to this day, we call them ugly biscuits. They are a

* Southern vernacular, page 139

Grandson Jasper in the kitchen with Danna.

family favorite, and I have given the recipe out many, many times. I have cooked them for family, friends, state lawmakers, and dignitaries from huge companies—and they always ask for the recipe.

Well, I digress. Back to my hungry soldier who was on survival training with very little rations. He told anyone who would listen about how good my ugly biscuits were. He was so hungry, he even dreamed about them, bless his hungry heart. And you better believe, when I flew across the country to see him after his training was completed, my biscuit pan was in my suitcase! Every good cook knows that the pan makes the difference. I got to tell you, I got some funny comments when going through security at the airport, but they just got to know how we Southern mommas think. My son was hungry! And if my son wants my ugly biscuits, he's going to get some—I'm going to feed that boy or die trying!

It brought much joy to my heart to be able to feed him again. To have his boots under my table before he left (even if it was a rented cabin) and to watch him savor those biscuits made my momma-heart so happy. He needed those ugly biscuits to go out and serve his country, and I needed to feed him and cherish my time with him before I sent him back to serve.

National security, a momma's heart, and ugly biscuits...God Bless America!

Ugly Biscuits

By Danna Standridge

2 cups self-rising flour
1 stick butter, melted
2 tablespoons butter
1 cup milk
1 tablespoon vinegar

Preheat oven to 475°.
Pour vinegar into milk and set aside till needed.
Place 2 tablespoons butter in bottom of skillet and place in oven to melt.
Place flour in mixing bowl and make a well/indentation in the center.
Pour in the milk/vinegar mixture into the well in the flour.
Pour in the melted stick of butter.
Stir together. Batter will be thinner than traditional biscuit dough.
Drop large spoonfuls onto prepared buttered skillet every 2 inches.
The batter will spread and slowly connect as it cooks.
Bake for 10-14 minutes till bottom is crisp and brown and top is lightly brown.
Cut biscuits apart.

Nanny Swann's Famous Chicken-n-Dumplings: A Quest for Culinary Excellence

We Alabamians love our God, our mommas, our family heritage, and our food! No doubt about it! We've been loving them for nigh onto 200 years. We eat at Church dinners, respect our mommas, treasure items from our family heritage, and hand down our best family recipes from generation to generation. And heaven forbid*, if we somehow don't have the recipe written down (as many of our wonderful mommas and grandmas kept their recipes safely tucked away in their creative and loving minds), we spend years trying to formulate the exact recipe to get that just-so-special feeling we always got when we ate our loved ones' food. It's true! We are just that dedicated to our culinary heritage.

* Southern vernacular, page 139

As a little girl, I remember looking forward to Sunday dinner at my Nanny Swann's. Boy, could she cook! There is a long list of dishes we all devoured and enjoyed, but she was renowned for her chicken and dumplings in our family and at our church dinners. Everyone's mouth would start watering just thinking about them during the Sunday morning preaching. When we headed to the fellowship hall after service, many would ease up to her and say, "Lorene, did you bring your dumplings?"

Recently, I've turned into a culinary detective in my quest to accurately recreate my

Danna with her granddaughter, Leah

Four generations making Nanny's dumplings: From left, Leah, Danna, Lonna, Shirley.

Nanny Swann's dumplings. Years ago, my mother, Shirley Swann, questioned Nanny about her dumpling recipe to put into a church cookbook. That became my jumping-off point of culinary excellence in Southern dumpling-making. Using this recipe, I made them and they were good, but they weren't Nanny's dumplings. So, I questioned my Aunt Janet (Nanny Swann's daughter) and she wrote down helpful hints. I made more dumplings. They were very good, but they still weren't exactly right.

What does a Southern girl do when you need a little help with an issue? You call your momma. My momma and I got together and made two big pots of dumplings with slightly different recipes. We parceled both out to people we knew had eaten many of Nanny's dumplings. When the vote was in, we had an acceptable working dumpling recipe. The dumpling itself was exactly right, but the broth was still not exactly how I remembered it.

Then, fortuitously, my cousin Rose contacted me. She had heard I was in dumpling making mode, and she was also trying to recreate our beloved Nanny's dumplings. She remembered a conversation in which Nanny told her how she made her dumplings, so we compared notes and made adjustments. I made more dumplings and sent them out for family to taste. Eureka, we had done it!

And now, after much ado and experimenting, I present to you, my Nanny Swann's Famous Chicken and Dumplings!

Nanny Swann's Chicken and Dumplings

Recipe of Lorene Thomas Swann by her granddaughter Danna Lorene Swann Standridge

Nanny would cook her dumplings before church and turn off the heat and cover with a lid. Dumplings would be wonderful after coming in from Sunday morning church. Now if the preacher went long, as happened sometimes, and the dumplings got too thick, Nanny would add a little water and turn the heat on low and give them a gentle stir to get them ready for the Swann family.

Preparing Your Chicken:
Place 3 lbs. cut-up chicken with skin into pan. Cover with water 1 inch over top of chicken, approximately 8-10 cups. Add 1/2 tablespoon salt to water. Place over medium heat, bring to low boil, turn to low simmer till chicken is tender and pulls from bone easily, about 45 minutes. Remove chicken from water and let it cool. Discard skin and bones. Shred chicken. Set aside. Keep broth to cook dumplings in.

Making Dumplings:
2 cups plain flour
1 teaspoon salt
1/2 stick butter, melted
1/2 to 2/3 cup warm broth from stewing your chicken

Put flour and salt in bowl, make well in center, add 1/2 cup broth and melted butter, stir, and gradually add broth as needed till dough forms a ball. If dough is too wet, add more flour. If too dry, add more broth. Let dough rest for 15-20 minutes.

Flour counter and work dough to a smooth ball being careful not to overwork the dough. Overworking will cause tough dumplings. Divide dough into 2 pieces. Flour counter and roll dough to 1/8" thick. Cut into dumplings the size of your choice. Nanny's were about 2"×1 1/2".

Cooking Dumplings:
saved broth and chicken from above
1/4 teaspoon black pepper
1 cup whole milk
2 tablespoons flour

Bring chicken broth to a rolling boil. Drop 3 to 4 dumplings in one at a time in different areas of the broth so they won't stick to each other. DO NOT OVER STIR. Adjust heat as necessary to keep dumplings from scorching. After last dumpling is added cook for at least 10 minutes at a gentle rolling boil. Add 2 cups of shredded chicken and 1/4 teaspoon black pepper to the broth. Whisk 2 tablespoons of flour to one cup of whole milk and pour into the broth. Bring back to a gentle boil for 10 minutes. Turn off heat. Put the lid on and let sit for 15 minutes or more until the juice has thickened to your liking.

Jasper calling from the old family phone, which can be traced from him back through seven generations of Danna's family.

Oh Nooooo... Not the Gravy!

Ruby and Hayden Holt, also known as Moma and Pop Holt, 1934

When you happen upon a family gathering, a good part of the conversation starts with a bygone story about food: "Remember when..." and then we get told (for the umpteenth time* as Moma Holt would say) how old Uncle So-and-So (names have been changed to protect the guilty) spilled the gravy all over the floor at one of our traditional day-after-Thanksgiving breakfasts.

How did it happen? Well, my wonderful mother-in-law, Patty Holt Standridge, who is known as Aunt Patty at the Holt family get-togethers, makes the best sausage gravy on the planet just like her momma taught her. As a special annual treat on the day after Thanksgiving, Aunt Patty makes a huge batch of the sausage gravy, and Aunt Phyllis, her sister, makes her scrumptious biscuits.

At one particular Thanksgiving, Moma Holt, the matriarch of the whole 80 plus bunch, said, "Get your food ready, the gravy's almost done." So, we were all setting up the ham, turkey, bacon, sausage, scrambled eggs, biscuits, breakfast casseroles, coffee, jams, jellies, and fruit, when we heard a huge crash as the makeshift table holding the big bowl of gravy toppled to the floor. We all stopped and slowly turned to see the most horrifying sight a hungry Southerner could ever witness. You could have heard a pin drop as all eighty pairs of eyes became glued to the sight of Aunt Patty's delicious gravy slowly spreading all over the floor amongst the rubble of the broken bowls and broken platters filled with meat and eggs.

Taking stock of the situation Moma Holt hollered with anguish, "It's ruined! It's ruined! The whole meal is ruined!"

Right on her heels, Cousin Cory yelled out what we were all thinking: "OOOHHHHH NNNOOOOO! Not the gravy!!!"

Lord, y'all, it was a big ol' mess!! Food was everywhere! All over the floor—gravy, eggs, meat, and lots of grease! So, Aunt Patty, cousin Karen and I worked as clean-up crew while Aunt Phyllis and the other sisters went back to the kitchen to cook up some more breakfast. But, y'all, we were clean out of sausage. There would be NONE of Aunt Patty's sausage gravy that year. None. Not a drop. We had to make do with what was left after all the meat, eggs, and gravy were cleaned up and thrown out. We were devastated, to say the least.

We Alabamians have been taught from a young age to be kind and to sympathize with folks who find themselves in a bad situation. Never make a person feel bad if a bad thing happens to them. Just be kind. So, after the initial shock had worn off, we had an uproar of conversation amongst ourselves to find out what happened to our gravy and who was the culprit while trying to not make him feel bad. We learned that Old Uncle So-and-So had leaned onto the makeshift table, causing it to tump over*, taking Aunt

* Southern vernacular, page 139

Patty's delicious homemade gravy crashing to the floor.

Well, this was a terrible, terrible thing that happened to Uncle So-and-So! We commiserated with him on his accident and checked on his aches and scratches from the fall, thankful that the hot gravy didn't land on him. And, we were still nice to him, you know... and he's not really blood-kin, after all...and he is a very good fellow, but we were completely devastated! To this day, if he is not in the room, and sometimes just because he is in the room, someone will always say, "Remember when Old Uncle So-and-So spilled the gravy?..."

And, just so you know, we keep a careful watch on Old Uncle So-and-So when we are having gravy—just saying.

Moma Holt's Sausage Gravy

By Patty Holt Standridge

1 lb. sausage
1/2 cup flour
1/2 cup bacon grease or cooking oil
1 teaspoon salt
1/2 teaspoon pepper
2 cups water added to 1 can evaporated milk*

Put bacon grease in skillet over medium heat and cook sausage in it until it is brown. Stir in flour, salt, and pepper. Cook flour till a tan color, stirring constantly. Pour milk into pan, stirring constantly. Turn heat to low so it will simmer slowly till thickened. If it gets too thick, stir in a little milk.

For the best gravy flavor, put it in a *warm* crock pot and let it simmer for at least 30 minutes before serving.

*Evaporated milk adds a silky creaminess to the gravy and is sold in small cans in the baking section of the grocery store. However, 2 1/2 cups of regular milk can be substituted if you don't have evaporated milk.

Apple Sauce ...

1 large Egg
2 tablespoons Vegetable oil
1 1/2 Cups ...
2 Cups unsweetened applesauce
3/4 teaspoon ...
2 teaspoons ...
1/2 teaspoon ...
1/2 teaspoon ...
3/4 Cups ...
Pinch of ...

Pork Chop Skillet Di...

2 tablespoons ...
6 (1/2-inch-th...
3/4 teaspoon ...
1/2 teaspoon ...
6 Sm...
1 (10...

Chicken ...

2 to 3 Cups Cooked chicken
4 Hard Boiled eggs chopped
2 Cups Cooked Rice
1 1/2 Cup chopped Celery
1 Small onion chopped
1 Cup Mayonnaise
2 Cans Cream of Chicken soup
1 - 3 oz pkg ...

Salads & Soups

SALADS

Scrumptious Layered Salad

1 head lettuce, washed and prepared
2 bell peppers, chopped
1 onion, finely chopped
1 can English peas, drained (I use Le Sueur, 15 oz)
1 cup mayonnaise
1 cup sour cream
1 envelope Hidden Valley Ranch Dressing
Parmesan cheese
bacon bits

Mix together the mayonnaise, sour cream, and ranch dressing. Set aside.
Layer in a glass dish (this is a beautiful salad) as follows:
Lettuce, bell pepper, onion, English peas.
Now, spread the mayonnaise mixture over it.
Sprinkle on the Parmesan cheese.
Sprinkle the bacon bits on top.

Orange Fluff Salad

1 12 oz cottage cheese
1 10 oz Cool Whip
1 box orange Jell-O
1 can crushed pineapple, drained

Stir the pineapple and Jell-O together thoroughly making sure the sugar from the Jell-O dissolves.
Stir in the cottage cheese till well-combined.
Stir in the Cool Whip.
Chill and serve.

Beth's Cornbread Salad

1 skillet of cornbread, crumbled
1 bell pepper
1 cup mayonnaise
large jar of sweet relish
1 cup tomatoes, diced
1 lb. bacon, cooked
1 onion, finely chopped
1/4 cup vinegar
1 tablespoon sugar

Crumble cornbread .
Chop your bell pepper, onion, tomatoes, bacon, and mix together.
Put a layer of cornbread, then layer of vegetables and bacon mix. Repeat layering until all is used.
Mix mayonnaise, vinegar, sugar, and sweet relish, juice and all.
Pour over the cornbread mixture.
Cover and let stand in the refrigerator.
Mix well before serving.

Suzanne's Broccoli Salad

3 to 4 cups fresh broccoli
1 cup raisins (dried cranberries can be used for raisins)
1 cup toasted sunflower kernels
1 cup green onions, chopped
1 cup mayonnaise
3 tablespoons balsamic vinegar
1/2 cup sugar
4 to 5 slices bacon

Mix mayonnaise, vinegar, and sugar.
Cook bacon and crumble.
Mix broccoli, raisins, and onions with the mayonnaise mixture.
Refrigerate 2 to 3 hours.
Toss with bacon and sunflower seeds before serving.

Green Bean Salad

Salad Ingredients:
1 can green beans
1 can English peas
1 large onion, chopped
1 bunch celery, chopped
2 pimentos
salt (to taste)

Salad Directions:
Drain all cans.
Mix all ingredients together and salt to taste. Let stand.

Dressing Ingredients:
1/2 cup oil
1 1/2 cup sugar
1 cup vinegar
1/2 teaspoon paprika

Dressing Directions:
Mix all together.
Pour over salad and let stand 24 hours.

Moma Holt's Potato Soup

A basic potato soup recipe. To feed more people, add more potatoes, butter, flour, milk, and seasoning to suit your tastes.

3-4 lbs. potatoes
salt and pepper (to taste)
butter (to taste)
1/2 cup milk
2 tablespoons flour

Peel and dice up potatoes.
Put in a pot and cover with water.
Cook until potatoes are done.
Add salt, pepper, and butter to taste.
Mix milk with flour, whisk with a fork, and pour into soup.
Stir until lumps are gone and it thickens up.
Taste the soup and add more salt, pepper, and butter to suit your taste.

Shrimp and Bean Soup

1 large onion, chopped
1 tablespoon olive oil
2 14 oz cans reduced sodium chicken broth
2 10 oz cans Ro-tel tomatoes with green chilies, undrained
2 cups frozen corn
1 can black beans, drained and rinsed
1 can diced tomatoes, undrained
4 1/2 teaspoons chili powder
1/2 teaspoon salt
1 teaspoon sugar
1 pound uncooked medium shrimp, peeled and deveined
1/4 cup parsley, minced

In Dutch oven, sauté onion in olive oil for 3 to 4 minutes until tender.
Add broth, Ro-tel tomatoes, corn, black beans, tomatoes, chili powder, sugar, and salt and bring to a boil, stirring occasionally.
Reduce heat and cover and simmer for 20 minutes. Stir in shrimp.
Cook 5 to 6 minutes till shrimp turns pink.
Stir in parsley.
Keep refrigerated

Spicy Chicken-Tomato Pantry Soup

Delicious and spicy and very quick to make with staples from the pantry. The first time I made it, David liked it so much that I stopped eating and immediately wrote down this recipe.

1 Tablespoon chopped jalapenos
12 oz. can chicken with juice
14 oz. can diced tomatoes
½ cup water
Salt and pepper to taste
Pinch of red pepper flakes
½ teaspoon cumin
2 teaspoons dried oregano
1 ramen noodle block (discard flavor packet)
¼ cup sour cream
½ cup shredded cheddar cheese
½ cup parmesan cheese

Add ingredients #1-8 into saucepan over medium heat. Bring to a boil. Add #9 but discard the flavor packet. Cook for 3 minutes. Stir and remove from heat. Add ingredients # 10-12 and stir. It's ready to serve.

Venison Stew with Veggies

2 bay leaves
1 tsp. of each of the following: herb de Provence, turmeric, garlic powder
1/4 teaspoon cayenne
Salt and pepper to taste
2 Tablespoon Olive oil
1 Tablespoon Worcestershire sauce
1 lb. stew meat, venison or beef
1 lb. soup vegetables, frozen
1 can tomato paste
1 can Rotel
1 large can diced tomatoes
1 sliced smoked bacon, chopped

Brown the meat in olive oil. Add all the spices and the remaining ingredients.

If using a: **Dutch oven:** Bring to a boil, then turn to low simmer on the stovetop for three hours. **Crock Pot:** Cook on low all day for eight hours. Instant Pot: Pressure for 25 minutes with a slow release.

Danna and grandson J.D. Dillard making cornbread.

One Alabama Family's Culinary Heritage and Adventures

Part 3

Facing Tough Times with Southern Ingenuity

Alabama has seen many glory days, for which we are thankful. However, with Southern tenacity, true grit, and determination, we have also made it through some mighty tough times. The War Between the States, better known as the Civil War, was a very dark time for our nation and for our state, as were World War I and World War II, to name a few. As a mother who has sent her son off to war, my heart hurts for the many lost during those times, and I pray for peaceful times with my family gathered happily around my table.

During these hard times, those on the battlefields fought for their families while those on the home front did their best to feed their families. In many cases, food was rationed or was not to be found at all. Cooks in Alabama used their ingenuity to feed their families the best way they could. My Great-Aunt Sue Parker Shipp tells about some dishes enjoyed by her family when she was a little girl in which syrup and molasses were sometimes used to replace sugar, and another one where a regular biscuit recipe was turned into a mouthwatering butter roll dessert for hungry families.

Aunt Sue had a syrup cake recipe, but she didn't have the recipe for a butter roll. Her granddaughter found one that is very similar to what Aunt Sue remembers her mother using in that Alabama kitchen so long ago. It is by far one of the best things I've ever put in my mouth!

Opposite: World War II and the John Parker Family. From left, Loyd and friend in uniform, letter to family from U. S. Government telling them their son was missing. Only later did they find he was a prisoner of war in Germany; Loyd's older brother, Aves, with the family mules; letter from Loyd to his mother; the Parker family with Loyd at his homecoming celebration.

Butter Roll Dessert

As told to Danna Standridge by Sue Parker Shipp

biscuit dough
1 stick butter, softened
1 cup sugar, divided
1 teaspoon cinnamon
2 cups milk
1 teaspoon vanilla

Make your biscuit dough and roll flat.
Spread butter on dough. Sprinkle 1/4 cup sugar and 1 teaspoon cinnamon.
Roll up and slice.
Place in greased skillet.
In a sauce pan, mix 2/3 cup sugar, 2 cups milk, 1 teaspoon vanilla.
Heat over medium heat, stirring constantly, till mixture begins to bubble lightly. Pour over the rolls in the pan.
Bake for 30-40 minutes at 350° or until rolls are lightly browned on top.

Sue said her momma made small individual rolls and didn't slice them so they each had a little roll of their own.

Danna's father-in-law, Jack Standridge, driving the children in the old Swann family wagon.

Sorghum Syrup Skillet Cake

By Sue Parker Shipp

3/4 cup sugar
1/2 cup butter, softened
1 egg
1 teaspoon vanilla
3/4 cup evaporated milk
2 cups self-rising flour
1 cup sorghum syrup or molasses

Cream together the sugar and butter.
Mix in egg and vanilla.
Add milk and flour alternately and blend well.
Blend in syrup.
Pour into lightly greased 10 inch cast iron skillet.
Bake at 350° for 1 hour or until cake tests done.

Granny Dera's Christmas Candy — Learning Our Culinary Lesson

Julius and Dera Standridge, 1959

Our Southern grannies are such jewels! We love, honor, and cherish them for their wisdom, wit, and knowledge. We eat good when our shoes are under their table, too. And, they sure do love their grandchildren—Lord, yes*—they really do love with a mighty big heart! But just because they love us doesn't mean they don't give us a good lesson every now and again in amongst all the feedings.

Now, Granny Dera was one of the best cooks around. We always loved eating her good cooking. Some of my best memories of my husband's grandmother, Dera Standridge, are her sweet potato pies, candied yams, divinity, and fried apple pies.

On Christmas Day every year, David and I would load up our three children and go see Granny Dera around midday. We would take her a Christmas present, and she would pull out all kinds of her homemade treats. She spent a lot of time making delicious goodies for her numerous children and grandchildren to enjoy throughout the holidays. It was a joy to visit with her at Christmas time, and we sure did devour her goodies. Needless to say, our healthy eating plan was shot...but we looked forward to it every year with joy and gusto!

Now, our Christmas routine for years was very scheduled. David and I were both blessed with large families on all sides with lots of aunts, uncles, and cousins to love. When we first got married, we had nine Christmas stops to make! Many of our great-grandparents were still living at the time, and we visited them all at Christmastime with lots of hugs, kisses, and presents to open, surrounded by big families loving on all the babies. (And if you disappointed them and didn't appear at their Christmas event, you heard about it later, too! Major guilt trip, just saying.)

Yes, we were truly blessed to have many generations to visit. It was a scheduling feat to drive to all of these family get-togethers over the course of Christmas Eve and Christmas Day. With all our many grandmothers and grandfathers, we would spend both days taking them their gifts and enjoying their cooking. And you couldn't miss a one! Heavens no! It was frowned upon and considered disrespectful towards our grandparents if we didn't grace them with our presence at the allotted time at Christmas. How they would fuss over us and love on us. Oh, how I miss those days!

One year, things "took a turn*." Our plans were unexpectedly altered. On Christmas Eve, we found that Granny Dera was at our Christmas Eve breakfast at David's mom and dad's house. Well, we scurried home and got her gift so she could enjoy it as we all opened our gifts. She loved the gift, and we enjoyed her delectable treats after the commotion of all the gifts being given and received. There you go—one less place to visit on Christmas Day—or so we thought.

* Southern vernacular, page 139

We thought we were in good with Granny Dera until along about March of that year on her birthday visit. We had visited with her at David's parents' house on several occasions since the holidays, and we thought everything was just fine and dandy*.

But on her birthday when we went to her house to visit, she lowered the boom on us. Granny Dera said that on Christmas Day, she missed us so bad and waited and waited all day for us to come visit. When we didn't show up, she told herself she would just save the homemade goodies for us to eat when we did finally come for a visit.

So, she took those three-month-old goodies out of the pantry and served them right up to us. And let me tell you, we ate with as much gusto as we could manage considering that they were made three months ago! A little stale, yes indeed, and a little off-tasting, yes, they were, but we didn't know if we would ever get on her good side again, so we were eating that stale candy for all we were worth. But, after a few bites, we knew all was forgiven when she pulled out one of her wonderful, freshly made, delectable sweet potato pies and sent it home with us with lots of hugs and kisses. Granny Dera was famous for her sweet potato pies.

It's funny how our Southern grannies can teach us a lesson. They got the knack for delivering lessons that you won't forget! We left there with a vow that we would NEVER, EVER miss another Christmas Day visit with Granny Dera ever again! No matter how many other events she showed up at during the holiday festivities! And we never did.

Granny Dera's Sweet Potato Pie

By Dera Davidson Standridge

3 cups sweet potatoes
3 cups sugar
1 teaspoon vanilla
dash of nutmeg
1 stick butter
4 eggs, beaten
6 1/2 oz evaporated milk
2 uncooked pie shells

Boil sweet potatoes in their jackets until done.
Peel and mash. Add butter, sugar, vanilla, and nutmeg.
Combine eggs and milk. Mix with sweet potatoes until blended.
Pour into pie crust. Bake at 350° for 1 hour 20 minutes.

* Southern vernacular, page 139

Overthinking Football Can Get You in Hot Water

As a citizen of the great state of Alabama and with my family roots running all the way back to the 1800s, I marvel at the resilience and hardiness of its people, the caring attitude for their fellow man, and yes, their savage devotion to their football teams. People all over the world know of the rivalry between Alabama and Auburn. When my husband and I are in other parts of the country, invariably we will hear either an exuberant "Roll Tide!" or a "War Eagle!" when folks find out we live in Sweet Home Alabama, because people in other parts of the country root for one or the other, too. When fall weddings are planned, we check our football schedule to see if it will interfere with our football games. I'm not kidding!

Top: Auburn University's mascot, Aubie at the State House. War Eagle!

Bottom: Roll Tide Roll! with University of Alabama's mascot, Big Al.

During my teaching career in the high school classroom, I soon discovered that no teaching would be done until this question was settled: "So, who do you go for? Alabama or Auburn?" I taught six classes a day, and inevitably during the first week, someone would always put me on the proverbial spot.

Now, being a caring teacher who wanted all my students to succeed, and living in the state of Alabama with our savage devotion to either Alabama or Auburn, I debated on whether I should answer that question. Oh, the harassment that could ensue as a result. We Alabamians are very avid sports fans as I stated earlier.

As far as that goes, I support and have family members who attended both Alabama and Auburn, and I am proud to have them in our state. I'm one of the state citizens who support both universities, and I keep my mouth shut when they play each other.

Now, it wasn't always this way. I was raised an avid Alabama fan. I watched the games and got the t-shirts, and I still dearly love the Crimson Tide to this day. (Roll Tide!) However, after teaching in the classroom for ten years, I received a job offer to work in youth development in Blount County for the Alabama Cooperative Extension System, which is a division of Auburn University. I came to know and love Auburn and still do to this day. (War Eagle!) Both universities contribute so very much to our state and the well-being of our students that I am truly honored to support both universities. Believe it or not, it is possible to love them both!

So, you may ask, what did you tell the students? How did you answer that question? Well, after careful thought and consideration, I told my classes that I didn't graduate from Alabama or Auburn. My husband, our daughter, and I graduated from Athens State University (Go Bears!), which does not have a football team. My oldest son graduated from the United States Air Force Academy (Go Falcons!), and my youngest son graduated from Mississippi State as a veterinarian (Go Bulldogs!). So, my heart and

Danna's grandson Wyatt Dillard running the ball.

my money support the Falcons and the Bulldogs. Pretty safe answer, right?

Yes, I thought that was such a smart answer and would cover all my bases. No one should cause me grief during football season. The Falcons don't play SEC teams, and at the time, the Bulldogs weren't tough competition. To tell you how it was, when my son was heading off to college at Mississippi State, I had to sit him down and have the "talk." You know the one—"Sorry son, but you got to get used to not winning all the football games. They play our state teams and usually don't win. All your friends you graduated with are attending our state universities. They will harass you during football season. Are you going to be able to handle that?"

He felt certain he could handle it and was going in with his eyes wide open. But what I didn't expect was, Mississippi State beat UAB, Alabama, and Auburn!!! The Bulldogs' game had really improved! So, my son got the pleasure of bragging to his friends, and I took constant and continued grief at school from my students and fellow teachers for the whole duration of football season! (I even took my Mississippi State Veterinary School tag off my truck. I just felt it wasn't safe with the current intense situation, you know?) And, I just have to say, even with the best of intentions...overthinking football can really get you in hot water when you live in my sweet home, Alabama!

Supporting our cadet at the United States Air Force Academy football game: David, Gerald, Shirley, Joshua, Danna, Lonna, and Wes. Go Falcons!

One more football story and then I'm done: One young lady, bless her heart, planned her wedding on an intense game day when our teams were fighting major rivals. She was marrying an out-of-state guy so they were going by his football schedule. Tsk, tsk. We had to go because of our close work association with her. The game was on during the ceremony, and here we were, sitting in pretty little white chairs smack-dab* in the middle of a hay field, not a TV in sight. Folks were tense wondering what was happening in the game but trying to look like respectful wedding guests. Then, my friend in the row in front of me pulled out his cell phone—YES! He had a good signal!—and solemnly, without hooting or hollering, kept us up-to-the-minute on the game in a quiet whisper. (As I was saying earlier, we have been taught our manners.) The stress level dropped for all those around him, and I enjoyed the wedding and the game in a quiet and dignified manner. But I will say we made a fast get-away at the reception. They didn't even have the game on at the reception—can you believe it!?!

What ranks high on the list of every football fan in the state? Football food! All Alabama families have their own special "football food." When football season draws near, we dust off our winning recipes, stock the pantry, and get ready for the excitement and heated competition of the Alabama and Auburn football rivalry. We hoot and holler and talk a little trash as we usher in our beloved football season.

Man, I just can't wait for football season!

* Southern vernacular, page 139

Easy Cheesy El Gando

By Danna Standridge

Something's cooking with Danna and David.

2 lbs. ground beef
2 cans (14.5 oz) diced tomatoes
1 can Ro-tel, tomatoes and green chilies
1 package chili mix
1 package yellow rice
1 can cheddar soup
1/2 cup milk
1 cup grated cheddar
1 bag corn chips if serving as a main dish
OR, 1 bag tortilla chips if serving as layered dip

Cook and drain ground beef.
Add chili mix, tomatoes, and Ro-tel.
Simmer until almost dry.
Cook yellow rice as directed on package.
Heat cheddar soup and milk until blended and hot.
Layer the following in a 9"×13" casserole dish: 1/2 of meat/tomato mixture, all the yellow rice, remainder of meat/tomatoes.
Spread cheddar soup mixture evenly on meat and then sprinkle cheddar cheese on top.
If serving as a main dish—top with corn chips, or serve with tortilla chips for a layered dip.
Serves ten.

Main Dishes

CHICKEN & TURKEY

Lorene's Skillet-Fried Chicken

3 lb. fryer chicken
1 cup flour
2 teaspoons salt
1/4 teaspoon pepper
2 cups buttermilk
vegetable shortening or cooking oil

Melt enough shortening or oil in a large skillet so it is 1 1/2 inches deep and start heating it.
Mix flour, salt, and pepper into a shallow dish.
Pour buttermilk into shallow dish.
Coat each piece of chicken in flour, buttermilk, then flour again.
Place chicken in hot oil.
Cover and cook about 15 minutes or until golden brown.
Turn pieces over and reduce the heat.
Continue cooking uncovered until juice runs clear when pierced with a fork.
Drain and serve.

Southern Parmesan Chicken

2/3 cup instant potato flakes
1/3 cup grated Parmesan cheese
3/4 teaspoon salt
1/3 cup butter, melted
1 chicken, cut up and skinned

Heat oven to 400°.
Line your baking pan with aluminum foil for easy clean-up.
Combine potato flakes, Parmesan cheese, and salt.
Dip chicken in melted butter then roll in potato flake mixture to coat.
Bake for 35-45 minutes until chicken is fork tender, juices run clear, and crust is golden brown.

Mom's Comfort Chicken

2 jars dried beef
8 slices bacon
1 1/2 cans cream of mushroom soup
1 cup sour cream
paprika
8 chicken breasts, deboned

Line large oblong casserole dish with dried beef. Roll each chicken breast and wrap it with a slice of bacon. Place chicken on top of dried beef. Combine soup and sour cream and pour it over chicken. Sprinkle with paprika. Cover with foil. Bake for 3 hours at 300°. Remove foil for the last 30 minutes. Serves 8

Cheddar Cheese and Chicken Casserole

2 cups cooked chicken, cut up
2 cups cooked rice
1/3 cup chopped red bell pepper
4 oz can chopped green chilies
1/2 cup sour cream
2 cups shredded mild cheddar cheese, divided

Preheat oven to 350°.
Combine chicken, rice, pepper, chilies, sour cream, and 1 1/2 cups of cheese.
Cover and bake for 25-30 minutes.
Top with remaining cheese.

Jack and Pat Standridge with Phyllis and David

Broccoli and Chicken Casserole

1 large can chicken breast
1 bag frozen broccoli
1 can cream of chicken soup
3/4 cup sour cream
3 tablespoons butter
sliced cheese
1 sleeve Ritz crackers

Cook broccoli in microwave and place in bottom of dish.
Add chicken.
Mix sour cream and soup together and pour over chicken.
Crumble 1 sleeve Ritz crackers and place in melted butter.
Lay sliced cheese on top of soup mixture.
Put cracker and butter mixture over cheese.
Bake at 350° for 30 minutes.

Chicken Casserole

2 to 3 cups cooked chicken
4 hardboiled eggs, chopped
2 cups cooked rice
1 1/2 cups celery, chopped
1 cup mayonnaise
2 cans cream of chicken soup
3 oz slice almonds
2 tablespoons lemon juice
1 cup bread crumbs
2 tablespoons butter
broth or water, if needed to get desired consistency

Mix all together except the bread crumbs and butter.
Pour into a lightly greased casserole dish.
Place bread crumbs on top and dot with butter.
Bake at 350° for 40 minutes.

Remembering times gone by for Opal Ilene and Lonnie Campbell. The background is wallpaper from the bedroom Danna slept in as a child when she spent the night at Grandpa and Granny Campbell's farm.

I Can't Believe It's Not Beef! Turkey Chili

2 tablespoons olive oil to brown the meat in
1 lb. ground turkey, cooked and drained
1 small can mushrooms, drained
2 tablespoons Worcestershire sauce
1 small can tomato paste
1 can black bean, drained
1 can Ro-tel, diced tomatoes and chilis
1 can diced tomatoes
1 1/2 tablespoon chili powder
3/4 tablespoon cumin
4 shakes cayenne pepper, or 1/8 teaspoon
1 teaspoon of each of the following: sugar, oregano, garlic powder
1 tablespoon salt
1/2 teaspoon pepper
1 cup water
1 can chicken broth or beef broth
tortilla chips, sour cream, cheddar cheese, and jalapenos for serving

*Add a splash of strong brewed coffee for deeper flavor

Brown ground turkey in olive oil.
Add Worcestershire sauce and mushrooms.
Stir in tomato paste and cook over low heat for 3 minutes.
Stir in beans, tomatoes, and Ro-tel.
Add all spices and sugar.
Stir in broth and water.
Cook over low heat for 30 minutes.
Serve with tortilla chips, sour cream, cheddar cheese, and jalapenos.

Turkey Meatloaf

1 lb. ground turkey
3-4 pieces of bread
1/2 to 3/4 cup milk
1 teaspoon garlic powder
1 1/2 tablespoon Worcestershire sauce
1 egg
1 teaspoon mustard
2 tablespoons ketchup
oats (optional)*

Tear bread into pieces and soak in milk till soggy.
Gently squeeze milk from bread and add to ground turkey.
Add next 4 ingredients. Stir gently and do not overwork.*
Form into loaf and place in pan.
Top with ketchup.
Cover with foil and bake for 45 minutes at 375°.
Remove foil, add more ketchup if desired, cook 15 more minutes.
Let rest 10 minutes before serving.

*If mixture gets too soggy, add oats 1 tablespoon at a time till right consistency.

Grandsons Wyatt and J.D. Dillard helping in the kitchen.

BEEF

Kim's Sausage Roll

1 French loaf dough (found with canned biscuits)
1 lb. sausage or ground beef
1 cup shredded cheddar
1 cup shredded mozzarella
basil, oregano, garlic powder to taste

Cook sausage and drain.
Unroll dough and sprinkle with 1/2 of the sausage, cheddar, and mozzarella down the center length of the dough.
Add the rest of the sausage, cheddar, and mozzarella.
Fold the dough over and pinch the ends to close.
Sprinkle the basil, oregano, and garlic.
Bake in a preheated oven at 350° till bread is done and brown.
Let cool for 10 minutes.
Slice and serve. I serve it with warm spaghetti sauce for dipping.

Polynesian Steak

1 1/2 lbs. round steak, cut into bite size pieces
1/4 cup melted butter
1/2 cup flour
1/2 teaspoon salt
dash of paprika
1/2 to 1 teaspoon curry powder
1 1/2 cups milk
3 tablespoons ketchup
crushed pineapple, sliced bananas, chopped pecans, coconut, and mandarin oranges

Coat steak with flour.
Brown it in the melted butter.
In skillet, cook slowly till tender, about 1 hour
Gradually stir in milk as you stir.
Add seasonings and ketchup.

Simmer till thick and smooth, stirring constantly.
Serve over rice.
Top with crushed pineapple, sliced bananas, chopped pecans, coconut, and mandarin oranges.

Gran-Gran's Hot Tamales

Tamales:
5 lbs. ground beef
2 tablespoons cumin, can use up to 4-5 for added flavor
4 tablespoons chili powder, adjust to suit your taste
6 tablespoons salt
3 tablespoons cayenne pepper, adjust to your tastes
1 large onion, chopped
1 large green pepper, chopped
2 cups water
3 cups yellow cornmeal
small coffee filters for cooking

Sauce:
1 46 oz can tomato juice or V8
6 tablespoons chili powder

Mix first 5 ingredients.
Add bell pepper and onion to water.
Add water mixture to meat mixture and mix well.
Gradually add yellow cornmeal to meat mixture and mix well.
This will be a heavy mixture.
Shape into slender tamales.
Roll tamales in yellow cornmeal.
Wrap tamales with dampened coffee filters.
Fold over one end and leave the other end open.
For sauce, mix ingredients together and bring to a boil.
Fill large pot with tamales (I turn pot on its side to begin with)
Put pot upright and cover the tamales with the sauce.
Bring to a boil, reduce heat, place lid on pot, and simmer for 1 hour.
Makes 7 dozen hot tamales.
Can be frozen when cooled.

Southern Hamburger Pie

1 lb. ground lean beef or ground turkey
1 tablespoon flour
1/2 teaspoon pepper
1 5 oz can biscuits
1 1/2 cups cottage cheese
4 oz mushrooms, canned and drained
4 oz cream cheese
1/2 teaspoon cumin
1/4 teaspoon salt
1 egg
red pepper flakes

Cook meat and drain fat.

Add mushrooms and cream cheese.

Cook over low heat till cheese melts.

Stir in flour, salt, pepper, cumin

Split canned biscuits and pat into bottom of casserole dish.

Put meat mixture on top of dough.

Combine cottage cheese with beaten egg and spread over meat mixture.

Sprinkle with red pepper flakes.

Bake at 350° for 30-45 minutes.

Quick and Easy Lasagna

2 lbs. ground beef
Salt and pepper
1 package spaghetti mix
1 qt. Ragu sauce or your favorite sauce
1 jar mushrooms, sliced
2 cups grated cheddar cheese
2 cups grated mozzarella cheese
2 eggs
1 pint cottage cheese
6 slips lasagna noodles, cooked

Cook meat, drain.
Add spaghetti mix, salt and pepper to meat.
Add Ragu sauce and mushrooms.
Beat eggs, and mix together with the cottage cheese. Set aside for layering.
Layer the following in a casserole dish:
Half of the meat, noodles, egg mixture, grated cheeses.
Then add the remainder of the meat, noodles, egg mixture, grated cheeses.
Bake at 400° for 20-30 minutes. Let sit for 20 minutes before serving.

Moma Holt's Cabbage Rolls

hamburger meat
head of cabbage
sauerkraut
tomatoes, canned
salt and pepper
toothpicks

Pour sauerkraut into crockpot.
Soften cabbage leaves in boiling water.
Place meat in center of each leaf, add salt and pepper.
Roll cabbage around meat, tucking in the ends, and secure with a toothpick.
Lay on kraut in crockpot.
Repeat till all meat is used.
Pour tomatoes over the cabbage rolls.
Cook on high 4 hours, or low 6 hours.

Serve with cornbread.

Easy Cheesy Enchiladas

1 lb. ground chuck or lean ground beef
1 can refried beans
1 can mild enchilada sauce
1 can Ro-tel, diced tomatoes and chilies
flour tortillas
sour cream
2 cups Monterey Jack cheese, grated
2 cups cheddar cheese, grated
1/2 teaspoon cumin
1/4 teaspoon of the following spices: oregano, chili powder, salt

Brown meat, drain fat.
Add spices to meat.
Add the beans, 1/2 the enchilada sauce, Ro-tel.
Stir and heat over medium-low heat.
Fill and roll your tortillas and line your casserole dish (I use a 9"×13" dish) till filled.
Spread a layer of sour cream over the filled tortillas.
Sprinkle both cheeses over the dish. Drizzle remaining enchilada sauce over top.
Place in preheated oven at 350° for 30 minutes.

Sunday Best Pot Roast

3 lb. beef roast
2 cans beefy mushroom soup
3-4 carrots, cut in 1 inch pieces
3-4 potatoes, quartered
1 medium onion, whole
salt and preferred seasoning

If time permits, salt and season the roast the night before adding your favorite marinade, keep refrigerated.
Preheat oven to 350°.
Brown both sides of roast in a heavy skillet on top of stove.
Place roast in a covered skillet or Dutch oven and cook for 1 1/2 hours.
Pour soup over roast, add 1 soup can of water.
Add vegetables and season.
Cover and cook for about 1 to 1 1/2 hours until the meat is tender.

Cooking with the grands. From left, Leah, Wyatt, Danna and J.D.

Beef Tips and Gravy

1 family-sized package beef tips
1 tablespoon olive oil
2 cans golden mushroom soup
1 1/2 cups water
Salt (to taste)

In the morning, put all ingredients in the crock pot on low. Cook all day. Serve over rice or mashed potatoes or biscuits.

Stuffed Bell Peppers

4 large yellow bell peppers
1/2 to 1 lb. ground chuck
1 box seasoned rice pilaf or seasoned wild rice
1 can cream of mushroom soup

Clean bell peppers, and blanch for approximately 5 minutes.
Prepare rice according to package directions.
Brown and drain meat.
Combine cooked rice with the cooked meat, and stir in the soup.
Stir until combined.
Stuff peppers with this mixture.
Bake at 350° for 20 minutes.
I like to cut my peppers in half

Lillian's Hamburger Bean Casserole

1 lb. hamburger meat
1/4 lb. bacon
1/2 cup onion
1 can kidney beans
1 can green lima beans
1 can pork and beans
1/2 cup ketchup
1 tablespoon mustard
2 tablespoons vinegar
3/4 cup brown sugar
salt and pepper (to taste)

Combine the hamburger, bacon, and onion and fry all together in skillet.
Drain off fat.
Combine all remaining ingredients.
Add cooked meat to mixture.
Cook in oven at 350° for 1–1 1/2 hours or in a crock pot on low for 4 to 5 hours.

Great dish for church suppers.

Country Fried Steak and Gravy

Steak Ingredients:
1 lb. cube steak
2 cups buttermilk
1 cup flour
salt and pepper
cooking oil for frying

Steak Directions:
Pour cooking oil in a large skillet so it is 1 1/2 inches deep and start heating it.
Mix flour, salt, and pepper into a shallow dish.
Pour buttermilk into a shallow dish.
Coat each piece of steak in flour, buttermilk, then flour again.
Place coated steak in hot oil.
Cover and cook about 6 to 8 minute per side or until golden brown.
Reduce heat.

Continue cooking uncovered until juice runs clear when pierced with a fork.
Drain and serve.

Gravy Ingredients:
4 tablespoons pan drippings
2 to 3 tablespoons flour
Salt and pepper
1 cup of milk

Gravy Directions:
Heat drippings, stir in flour and continue stirring as you slowly add milk.
Keep stirring until gravy thickens.
Salt and pepper to taste.
Serve over steaks or biscuits.

Swiss Steak

2 lb. round steak
1 onion, chopped
4 tablespoons bacon grease or cooking oil
1 clove garlic
1 cup tomato sauce
1/4 cup flour
1/2 teaspoon thyme
salt and pepper

Cut the meat into four pieces and pound well on each side to flatten.
Mix the flour with the thyme, salt, and pepper and dredge meat.
Brown the steaks on both sides in the bacon grease.
Add chopped onions and garlic and sauté for 2 minutes.
Add tomato sauce and simmer for 2 hours.
To use the pan sauce for serving, remove the fat and pour sauce over steaks.

Tater Tot Casserole

2 lbs. lean ground beef or ground turkey
1 cream of chicken soup
1 small package tater tots

Pat uncooked meat into pan.
Spread undiluted soup over the meat.
Layer tater tots on top and bake at 350° for 1 to 1 1/2 hours.

Moma Holt's Beef Tips and Noodles

beef tips, however much you have
1 can cream of mushroom soup
egg noodles
salt (to taste)

Put beef tips and enough water to cook the noodles in pan.
Bring to gentle boil and cook till beef is tender.
Add salt to taste.
Add mushroom soup and noodles.
Cook till noodles are done.

Corned Beef and Cabbage

corned beef, 2 lb., cooked according to package directions and sliced
2 heads of cabbage, cored and roughly chopped
1/2 lb. bacon
1/2 stick butter or more
salt and pepper

In your large Dutch oven or skillet, cook bacon and set aside.
Heat 2 tablespoons bacon grease and 1/2 stick of butter in pan.
Add cabbage. Cover with lid.
Cook over medium heat, stirring occasionally for even cooking.
Salt and pepper to taste.
Add more butter should it seem dry.
When all is done to your liking, sprinkle bacon over cabbage and serve with sliced corned beef and a pan of cornbread.

Shirley's Saucy Pork Chops

6 pork chops
1 medium onion, thinly chopped
1 can cream of chicken soup
1/4 cup ketchup
2 teaspoons Worcestershire sauce
salt and pepper (to taste)
cooking oil

Season pork chops with salt and pepper.
In skillet, brown pork chops on both sides in small amount of oil.
Top pork chops with onion slices.
Combine remaining ingredients and pour over chops.
Cover and simmer until done, about 45 minutes.
Remove chops to platter and spoon sauce over chops.

Goes well with hot biscuits or served over rice.

Pork Chop Skillet Dinner

2 tablespoons cooking oil
6 pork chops, 1/2 inch thick
3/4 teaspoon salt
1/2 teaspoon pepper
6 small potatoes, unpeeled
10 oz frozen English peas
5 medium carrots, sliced
4 small onions, quartered
1/2 cup water

Brown the pork chops in oil.
Add the remaining ingredients.
Cook on simmer for 45 minutes.

Lorene's One Pot Meal

1 large head cabbage, quartered
3 medium potatoes, peeled and sliced
3 medium carrots, peeled and sliced
1 large onion, sliced
1 link Conecuh sausage, we use Cajun flavor
salt and pepper to taste

In a Dutch oven, layer potatoes, carrots and onions.
Place the quartered cabbage on top.
Cut sausage into 2 inch pieces and slice open. Place on top of cabbage.
Add 1 1/2 to 2 cups water and cover.
Cook over medium heat for 30 minutes till vegetables are tender.
Serve with cornbread.

Easy Bacon and Cheese Quiche

8 slices bacon, cooked crisp and crumbled
1 pie shell part baked
1/2 lb. cheddar cheese, grated
1 tablespoon flour
1/2 teaspoon salt
dash of nutmeg
3 eggs, beaten
1 3/4 cups milk

Reserve 2 tablespoons bacon.
Place remaining bacon in pie shell.
Add cheese.
Combine next 5 ingredients in bowl and mix well.
Pour over cheese.
Sprinkle reserved bacon on top.
Bake in a preheated oven at 325° for 35-40 minutes.
Cool for 25 minutes before serving.

Fabulous RiverWood Venison Tenderloin with Mushroom Cream Sauce

Tenderloin:
1 venison tenderloin
3/4 cup soy sauce
1/2 cup melted butter

Preheat oven to 400°.
Place tenderloin in shallow baking dish.
Mix soy sauce with melted butter and whisk and pour over tenderloin.
Bake 10-12 minutes*.
Remove from oven and cover with foil.
Let tenderloin rest for 10 minutes before serving.

*Do not overcook.

Mushroom Cream Sauce:
1 tablespoon butter
1 tablespoon olive oil
6 oz portobello mushrooms, sliced
1/2 teaspoon horseradish (optional)
1 cup heavy cream
salt and pepper (to taste)
2 tablespoons chopped fresh parsley

Melt butter in saucepan over low heat.
Add olive oil and mushrooms and sauté 5 minutes.
Add horseradish and cream, stirring constantly.
Remove from heat and stir in salt, pepper, and parsley.
Serve warm.

Venison Stroganoff

2 lbs. ground venison, can substitute ground beef
2 tablespoons olive oil
1/2 teaspoon garlic powder, use more or less to suit your taste
1/4 teaspoon ground mustard
1/4 teaspoon cayenne, optional
1/4 teaspoon pepper
2 tablespoons flour
1 large can sliced mushrooms, drained
1 can evaporated milk
1 cup sour cream

Brown meat in olive oil. Add spices, flour, and mushrooms. Stir well and cook 2 minutes while flour browns. Stir in evaporated milk until sauce thickens. Simmer on low for 20 minutes. Add a little water if it gets too thick.
Take off heat and stir in sour cream. Serve over egg noodles.

*If the mixture is too rich, add a little vinegar.
*Adjust your seasonings to suit your family's taste.

Venison Roast

large venison roast, bone-in
flour
bacon, thick cut
seasonings—salt and pepper
toothpicks

Season meat with salt and pepper.
(Optional: Make 2 slits in roast and place garlic clove)
Rub roast entirely with flour.
Cover roast with slices of bacon, use toothpicks to keep in place.
Fat from the bacon will prevent meat from drying out.
Place in a Dutch oven at 300°, uncovered.
Cooking time is about 25 minutes per pound

Beth and Phil's Shrimp Gumbo

1 1/2 cups crabmeat
3 quarts water
1 teaspoon lemon juice
salt and pepper
2 lbs. okra, sliced
2 onions, chopped
2 green pepper, chopped
4 tablespoons roux (recipe below)
2 lbs. shrimp in shells
2 bay leaves
1 small onion, cut in wedges
4 tablespoons bacon grease, divided
4 tomatoes, peeled and chopped
1/2 teaspoon crushed red peppers
reserved shrimp stock
salt, pepper, and thyme to your taste
hot, cooked rice

In a large Dutch oven, boil water with bay leaves, lemon juice, onion wedges, salt and pepper.
Wash shrimp and add to pot. Boil 2 minutes.
Peel shrimp and return shells to stock to use later. Put shrimp and crabmeat in refrigerator until ready to add gumbo.
Sauté okra in 2 tablespoons bacon grease in a heavy skillet. The okra will turn dark as it cooks. When okra is soft, transfer to a stew pot and add tomatoes. Stir and mix together well.
Clean skillet and heat remaining bacon grease.
Sauté the chopped onions, green peppers, and red pepper. When soft, add to the stew pot.

To make Roux:
1/2 cup melted butter
1/2 cup flour
Combine well and cook until golden brown in color.

In a saucepan, warm the roux.
Strain shrimp stock and stir into the roux. When well blended add to the large stew pot with the other ingredients. Bring to a boil and simmer for 1 1/2 hours, adding more stock if needed.
Taste it then adjust seasonings.
Simmer 1 to 2 hours longer. Add the shrimp and crabmeat. Cook for 15 minutes. Serve with rice.

Betty's Shrimp Chowder

1/4 cup butter
4 large onions, peeled and sliced
1 cup hot water
6 medium potatoes, peeled and cubed
1 tablespoon salt
1/2 teaspoon pepper
6 cups milk
2 cups sharp cheddar cheese, shredded
2 lbs. shrimp, peeled and deveined
3 tablespoons chopped parsley for garnish

In a 5-quart Dutch oven, over medium heat, melt butter, and cook onions till tender. Add water, potatoes, salt, and pepper. Reduce heat to low; cover and simmer 15 minutes or until potatoes are tender; do not drain. Meanwhile, in a 3 quart saucepan over low heat, heat milk and cheese, stirring often, until cheese is melted. Do not let it boil.
Add shrimp to potatoes and cook until pink and tender, about 3 minutes.
To serve: add the hot cheese mixture to the potato mixture and heat, do not boil

David's Oven Fried Fish

fish fillets, can use frozen if the fishing wasn't good that day
corn meal
salt and pepper (to taste)
Italian seasoning
cooking oil spray
1 egg

Preheat oven to 400°.
Mix corn meal, salt, pepper, Italian seasoning.
Dip fish in beaten egg, roll in corn meal mixture.
Place fish on pan that is sprayed with cooking oil.
Spray fish with cooking oil.
Bake at 400° for 25-30 minutes.
Broil for 4 minutes.

In the early days of marriage when David was in law enforcement and Danna was home raising kids, going fishing sure did help with the family grocery budget.

One Alabama Family's Culinary Heritage and Adventures

Part 4

Poke Salat, a 15-lb. Bible, and True Love: Surviving and Thriving in the Rural South

When it came to surviving through the ages in the rural South, my family worked hard to survive and thrive. Just like many other Southern families, we Swanns work. (It's a family trait, and we are always hard at work!) And as a little girl, sitting around the Swann table at Sunday dinner, I learned so many secrets to the family survival. So many stories passed down through the generations, and they all intertwine into a beautiful rendition of Southern life involving many things, including: poke salat, a fifteen-pound Bible, and true love.

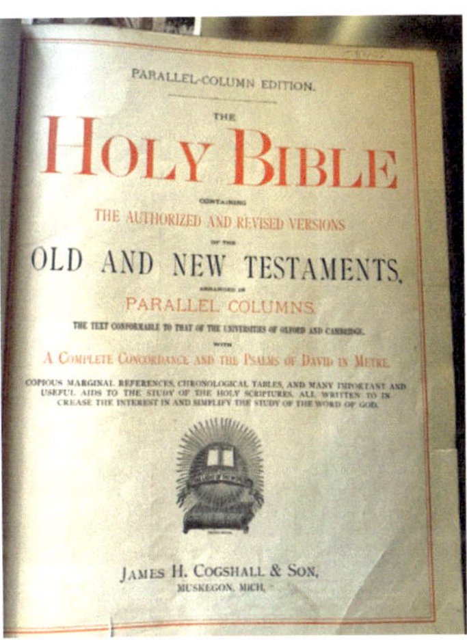

We Swann's call Alabama our promised land. When the forefathers were searching for a place to call home, Hayden, Alabama, was the chosen spot. The Swanns wanted a place to work and raise a family. And we did work with drive and determination and ingenuity in an effort to survive the times and contribute to the common good of mankind.

At eighteen years of age, Coy Swann was sweet on Lorene Thomas, his sixteen-year-old sweetheart. In 1928, Coy along with his younger siblings were to drive Lorene and her younger siblings to church in the family truck one Sunday morning in March. There were six people in that truck so it was crowded. But they never did show up for church that day. On that day, Coy whisked them off to a Justice of the Peace and married his beautiful sweetheart. That started a lifetime of love, family, and work which lasted for 67 years of wedded bliss.

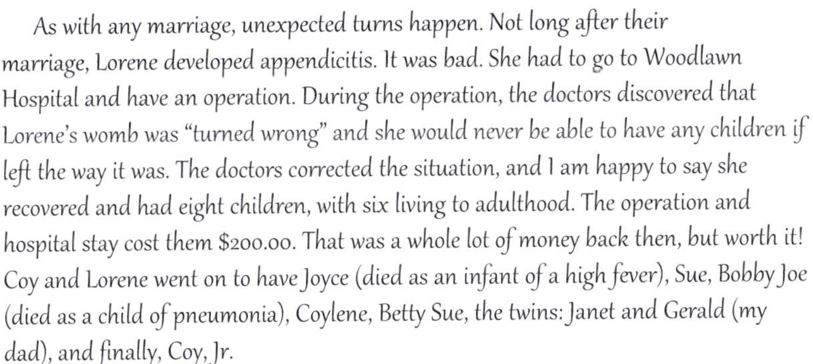

As with any marriage, unexpected turns happen. Not long after their marriage, Lorene developed appendicitis. It was bad. She had to go to Woodlawn Hospital and have an operation. During the operation, the doctors discovered that Lorene's womb was "turned wrong" and she would never be able to have any children if left the way it was. The doctors corrected the situation, and I am happy to say she recovered and had eight children, with six living to adulthood. The operation and hospital stay cost them $200.00. That was a whole lot of money back then, but worth it! Coy and Lorene went on to have Joyce (died as an infant of a high fever), Sue, Bobby Joe (died as a child of pneumonia), Coylene, Betty Sue, the twins: Janet and Gerald (my dad), and finally, Coy, Jr.

Now, Coy made his living as a farmer, and Lorene was right beside him. They raised cantaloupes and okra and took them to the Farmers Market to sale. Lorene worked on the farm and raised the children and cooked many wonderful meals for them. As a matter of fact, with her advice on cooking and child raising, she helped many a family, including mine.

Coy was very particular in how he raised his cantaloupes, according to his children who worked in the field with him. Everything had to be just right to get the best flavor in the crop. As they were working in the fields, it got long and sometimes they needed some entertainment. Yes, my dad, Gerald, would get up on a stump and preach to the family and give 'em a little bit of fire and brimstone, and the baby of the family, little Coy, Jr., would lead them in hymns (another family trait, we all sing.)

The Swann Family in 1967 Pictured from left to right, front row: Coy, Lorene, and Coy, Jr.; second row: Betty Sue, Coylene, Gerald, Sue, and Janet

As a farmer in the rural South, winter time was a time to venture out and find work elsewhere to help the family budget. Just like so many Southern families, Coy would get on the Greyhound bus and travel to Michigan to work. Lorene would stay in Alabama tending to all the children.

No matter where we Swanns go in the world, we trust in the Lord, and the good Lord takes care of us (another family trait). One winter day, Coy was walking to his job at a bakery in Michigan, and some men were tearing down a big three-story house. They yelled out to him, "Hey, do you want to buy a Bible?"

Well, it was a beautiful leather-bound and embossed Bible printed in the 1880s. And it weighed nearly 15 pounds! He bought it for $5.00, which was a lot of money back then, and brought it home to Alabama, and it's been a family treasure ever since. That year, 1951, Coy returned to sweet home Alabama with money for the family budget and a beautiful family Bible.

To make ends meet in feeding the family with an added benefit of serving as a health elixir, Poke Salat was the star of the spring! Every April, Southern families would be on the lookout for these delicious greens. They looked forward to it every year! At the Swann place, poke salat grew beside the spring where they got their water.

As in any family, time marches on. When my Dad, Gerald Swann, was sweet on my mother, Shirley Campbell, he invited her to eat with the family one fine spring day. He was so excited because his momma was going to cook the first batch of poke salat of the year. So, as they sat down to dine, all were eating the poke salat with relish, except for Shirley, not only was she nervous eating with the whole family for the first time, she didn't like poke salat! She had only taken a bite or two and was pushing it around on her plate. Lorene said, "Well, you must not like poke salat." "No, ma'am. My mother is the only one who eats it in our family."

While the Swann family loved poke salat, my mother's family, the Campbells, did not. However, that didn't deter my dad. He courted Shirley and won her over and she became his beautiful bride and raised four children together. And, every spring Shirley gathers and cooks poke salat for them both — because now, she likes it!

Poke Salat

as told to Danna Standridge

By Janet Swann Smithson and Shirley Campbell Swann

Gerald and Shirley's little ones, from left, Suzanne, Tommy, Dinah, and in the back is Danna.

Ingredients:
Poke Salat, gather a lot as they will cook down
Bacon
1 Onion, chopped
2 Eggs

To Gather Poke Salat: Gather the young leaves early in spring. Leaves are not to be eaten raw as they will make you sick.

Parboil: Chop the leaves finely. Add to large pan and cover with water. Boil it a little while until the water is green. Drain off the green water. Add more water and boil again for a little while. Drain off the green water.

Saute: Fry your bacon in a skillet. Remove when done and leave about 2 to 3 Tablespoons of grease in the pan. Add onions and saute until soft. Add the poke salat greens and saute until done. Break your eggs into a dish and whisk. Add to greens while stirring until the eggs set.

Serve with bacon.

The Turnip Green Ministry

Shirley and Gerald Swann

In the state of Alabama, recipes are not the only treasures handed down. Culinary ministries are handed down from generation to generation in some families, too. My Grandpa Campbell and his sweet wife, Stella, used to carry turnip greens to church and gift them to those they felt may be in need of the extra blessing a big ol'* pot of turnips greens can deliver. Now, I know what you are thinking, but I gotta say, don't knock it till you try it. Getting a big pot of greens and a skillet of cornbread can help you get back on your feet when life deals you a blow.

If you've ever picked and washed and cooked turnip greens, you know that it is quite a job. But it is a job well-worth the effort because of the deliciousness you get at the end. You can't just wash them once before you cook them. Those greens must pass through three or more washings before you cook them or you will end up with gritty greens. How do I know this? Well, let me tell you about my cousin. Early on in the first year of her marriage, she was determined to get a mess of greens* from the patch and cook them up for supper because she knew her husband loved turnip greens. She proudly served them up to her honey after he got home from work. He was really looking forward to them, but to her dismay, her poor husband spit out the first bite of greens she ever cooked him.

In the turnip green patch with Shirley.

He said, "Hon, how many washings did you put them through? It's full of grit!" Well, that lesson got learned, and I can tell you she's made many a wonderful pot of greens for her husband in the years they have been together since then. And after hearing her tell the story, I always make sure to put my greens through enough washes to get the grit off.

So you see, when someone brings you a pot of turnip greens, as a Southerner, we are very touched because we know the effort it takes to grow, gather, wash, and cook them. It's a touching tribute.

Now that my grandparents have passed on, my Momma and Daddy are carrying on the tradition of ministering to people in the community through their turnip green patch. They grow a patch every year with turnip greens and mustard greens. People know of my parents' generosity with their turnip greens and some come to pick 'em a mess of turnip greens. Others who are not able to go pick for themselves, who may be in need, who have suffered a loss of a loved one, or have suffered a setback in life will receive a good ol' pot of greens with my dad's delicious cornbread. Loving and caring for others through the turnip green ministry is a precious culinary tradition to me. And I cherish every bite!

The Turnip Green Ministry with Gerald and Shirley Swann, Molly and Buddy.

* Southern vernacular, page 139

Gerald's Cornbread

By Gerald Swann

3 tablespoons butter flavored Crisco
3/4 cup self-rising cornmeal
1/4 cup self-rising flour
1 egg
3/4 cup buttermilk
water as needed
6-inch cast iron skillet

Preheat oven to 475°.
Place Crisco into cast iron pan and put in the oven to melt as the skillet warms up.
Mix flour, cornmeal, egg, and buttermilk. Stir and mix well.
Next, stir in melted Crisco until blended well. Add water if it is too thick.
Pour into skillet.
Bake at 475° for 10 minutes or until bread is done.
Makes 4-6 servings.

Gerald's Turnip Greens

By Gerald and Shirley Swann

turnip greens, picked fresh
about 24 oz water
2 tablespoons bacon grease
3 chicken bouillon cubes
1 teaspoon salt

Take a bucket or foot tub, go to the turnip green patch and pick enough greens for a good meal. Wash greens through about 3 waters to make sure they are clean. Pick out any bad leaves.
Using a large pot with a lid, prepare the liquid to cook the greens.
Add about 24 oz water, bacon grease, bouillon cubes, and salt and bring to a low boil.
Place a few greens in at a time until all are in the pot.
Boil about 10 minutes, then turn to simmer and place a lid on top of pan and cook about 30 minutes or longer if needed.

The Very Blessed Turnip Green Patch

During the Great Depression, and when her house had just a few children, Moma Holt lived down the country road from her own mother, Grandma Thrift. As always, being the smart ladies that they were, they were looking for ways to survive and thrive during this difficult time in the South. So, each planted a turnip green patch at their house at the very same time.

Now, even though one raised the other, they both had different philosophies in how to manage their patch. Grandma Thrift, as her name implied, was quite thrifty and only did for her own. Now she was a good woman, but in her thinking, if others wanted turnip greens, they should have planted some just like she did. So, when the neighbors got hungry and came-a-calling* for a mess of greens* the answer was, "Nope, I'm saving those for us. I'll tend them, pick them, cook them and can them for my family. They will carry us through this tough time."

But, Moma Holt had an entirely different philosophy. She had a very sharing heart. As she was planting her patch, she prayed and asked God to bless it. When her hungry neighbors came-a-calling, her thoughts were, "Since God has seen fit to bless my little patch with turnip greens, I'm going to share them with others!" So, her answer was, "Why sure, pick yourself a mess of greens! Always glad to help a neighbor!"

And you know what? She had a very busy turnip green patch because food was scarce and her neighbors were all trying to make it through the Depression just like she was. She never turned anyone away. She didn't want anyone to go hungry. The more the neighbors picked, the more those turnip greens flourished. Moma Holt said she never went to the patch that she didn't have enough for her own family.

God blessed her family and all her neighbors because she had a giving heart and prayed for His blessings as she sowed those seeds!

And what about Grandma Thrift's turnip green patch? They all died! She had to go to her daughter's house and gather hers from the very blessed turnip green patch.

* Southern vernacular, page 139

Side Dishes & Vegetables

Skillet Roasted Corn and Black Bean Salsa

4 ears of sweet corn*
2 bell peppers, chopped
1 jalapeno, seeded and chopped
2 cans Ro-tel with juice
1 can black beans, drained and washed
juice of 1 lemon
1 tablespoon chili powder
1/2 tablespoon cumin
salt and pepper (to taste)
1 teaspoon sugar

In a dry skillet over high heat, roast your ears of corn, turning often.
Let cool and cut the corn off the cob.
Add all ingredients to large mixing bowl.
Stir and taste and adjust seasonings as needed.
The longer it sits, the better it tastes.

*1 can of drained crisp corn can be substituted for fresh corn

Happy New Year Black-Eyed Peas

1 ham hock
3 cups water
3 cups chicken broth
1 lb. black eyed peas, dry
10 oz diced tomatoes with chilis
salt (to taste)

Rinse the peas and look them over for debris.
Cover them with water and soak overnight or 8 hours. Drain off water.
Place all ingredients in a large pot.
Bring to a boil over medium heat.
Reduce heat to simmer and cover.
Simmer for 2 to 3 hours or until peas are tender and the texture is to your liking.
Salt to your taste.
Serve with turnip greens and cornbread.

*These can be cooked in a crock pot on low for 6-8 hours.

Consommé Rice

1 can beef broth
1 can French onion soup
1 cup Uncle Ben's Original rice

Mix together.
Bake for 1 hour at 350°.

Fried Apples

4 Golden Delicious apples, sliced
4 tablespoons butter
1/4 cup sugar
dash salt
cinnamon, if desired

In an iron skillet on top of stove, melt butter.
Add sliced apples.
Sprinkle with salt and cinnamon.
Cook over medium heat.
Sprinkle sugar over apples.
As the apples cook, they become somewhat transparent.
Test for doneness, and adjust sugar before removing from heat.
Good for any meal, especially breakfast.

Peggy's Broccoli Casserole

1 12 oz carton cottage cheese
1 12 oz package chopped frozen broccoli
3 eggs
1/4 cup melted butter
3 tablespoons flour
1/4 lb. cheddar cheese, diced
salt and pepper (to taste)

Mix all ingredients together.
Cook at 350° for 1 hour.

Potato Pancakes

2 cups mashed potatoes
1 egg, beaten
1/2 cup flour
1/4 to 1/2 cup milk, as needed
1 medium onion, chopped
salt and pepper to taste
cooking oil

Mix potatoes, eggs, flour, and onion.
Add a little milk if mixture is too stiff.
Have iron skillet with oil on medium-high heat.
Bring a heaping spoonful of batter in hot oil for each pancake.
Flatten a little on top if necessary.
Fry on each side turning only once.
They will cook fast, and you may need to turn the heat down.
Drain on a paper towel.
Better if eaten hot from the pan.

Brown Sugar Carrots

1 lb. baby carrots
2 tablespoons brown sugar
2 tablespoons butter
salt and pepper
1/2 cup water

Bring carrots, water, butter and brown sugar to boil over medium high heat.
Turn to low and simmer 5-6 minutes. Turn back to high until water evaporates (5-6 minutes).
Remove from heat. Add salt and pepper.

Luke's Okra

1 lb. small, fresh okra
2-3 tablespoons olive oil
salt and pepper

Preheat oven to 450°.
Toss okra in olive oil and sprinkle liberally with salt and pepper.
Roast 35-45 minutes until crunchy.

Skillet Candied Sweet Potatoes

2 or 3 sweet potatoes
1/2 stick butter
1 1/4 cups sugar
1 cup water
1 teaspoon vanilla

Melt butter in skillet on stovetop.
Put sliced sweet potatoes, sliced pretty thick, in skillet.
Cover with sugar, and then pour water over this.
Add vanilla.
Cook over low heat until potatoes are tender.
Watch carefully. Cook until candied.
You may need to add more water if necessary.

Morgan's Green Bean Bundles

5 cans whole green beans, drained
bacon, thick sliced
I bottle Italian dressing

Cut bacon in half and use 1/2 slice per bundle.
Place bacon in hand and 1/4 can of green beans on bacon and wrap bacon around the green beans.
Place in rows in 9”×13” baking dish.
Drizzle with Italian dressing.
Bake at 350° for 2 hours.

Arkansas Green Beans

5 15 oz cans green beans, drained (do not use fresh)
8 slices bacon
2/3 cup brown sugar
1/4 cup butter, melted
7 teaspoons soy sauce, can use low sodium
1 1/2 teaspoon garlic powder

Preheat oven to 350°.
Put green beans in 9"×13" baking dish.
Cook bacon in microwave 2 minutes and lay on top of green beans.
Combine remaining ingredients in a small bowl and pour over the green beans.
Bake uncovered for 40 minutes.

Parmesan Roasted Green Beans

1 lb. fresh green beans
2 tablespoons olive oil
2 tablespoons grated Parmesan cheese
2 tablespoons panko bread crumbs
1/2 teaspoon salt

Preheat oven to 400°.
Combine all ingredients in a large bowl, toss to coat.
Spread beans on large rimmed baking sheet.
Roast 15-20 minutes, stirring half way through.

Rosemary Roasted Sweet Potatoes

2 large sweet potatoes
1/3 cup butter, melted
1/4 cup packed brown sugar
1 tablespoon chopped fresh rosemary
2 teaspoons grated orange rind
1/2 teaspoon salt

Peel sweet potatoes, cut up like French fries.
Combine butter and next 4 ingredients in a large sealable plastic bag.
Add potato sticks to bag.
Seal bag and shake to completely coat the potatoes.
Arrange on a greased baking sheet.
Bake at 400° for about 40 minutes or until tender and brown.

Gerald's Fresh Corn on the Cob

fresh corn on the cob with the shucks on*
butter
salt

Place corn on plate keeping the shucks on it.
Put in microwave.
Cook 3 minutes per cob, adjust time per your microwave.
Pull shucks back and the silks will come off with it.
Butter and salt it, and then get to eatin'.
Don't burn your mouth.

*If corn is already shucked, wrap it in a damp paper towel before cooking

Ms. Vera's Cheesy Corn Casserole

1 16 oz can of creamed corn
3/4 cup cornmeal
1 small can green chilies, chopped
2 eggs
1/2 cup oil
3/4 cup milk
1 cup grated cheese
salt (to taste)

Mix all the ingredients together.
Bake in an oiled pan at 350° for 45 minutes.

Sautéed Cabbage

1 head cabbage
olive oil
salt and pepper

Cut cabbage into fourths.
Cut out the core.
Slice to your preferred size. My family likes 1/2 inch.
Heat 3 to 4 tablespoons olive oil over medium high heat in Dutch oven or large pan on stovetop.
Add cabbage and salt and pepper and stir.
Stir every few minutes allowing for some browning to occur, then cover with lid.
Add oil as needed. Taste, and adjust seasonings.

Macaroni and Cheese

4 cups elbow macaroni
3 cups milk
16 oz Velveeta
1 cup cheddar cheese
1 teaspoon salt
1 1/2 sticks butter
1/3 cup flour
1 cup shredded 4 cheese
8 oz cream cheese
1 teaspoon pepper

Cook noodles until tender and drain.
Pour in a large baking dish or aluminum pan (1/2 pan).
Melt butter in skillet. Add flour, salt, and pepper gradually.
Stir in milk and make a white sauce. When thickened add the 4 cheese, the Velveeta and the cream cheese. Blend together.
Pour over macaroni and mix well.
Sprinkle cheddar cheese on top and bake at 400° until brown.

Tomato Grits

2 cups water
1 1/4 cups milk
1 teaspoon salt
1 cup quick-cooking grits
1/2 cup plus 1 tablespoon butter, divided
1/3 cup chopped green onions
4 oz Mexican flavored processed cheese
1/4 teaspoon garlic powder
2 1/2 cups shredded cheddar cheese, divided
10 oz can diced tomatoes and green chilies

Preheat oven to 350°.
In a saucepan, bring water and milk to a boil.
Add salt and slowly add grits as you stir and return to a boil.
Stir constantly for 1 minute. Reduce heat, cover, and cook for 3 minutes.
While stirring grits add the 1/2 cup butter and stir till melted.
Cover and cook for 3 to 5 minutes or until the grits are thick and creamy.
Remove from heat and set aside.

In a small skillet, sauté onions in remaining butter for 1 minute.
Add the Mexican cheese, garlic powder, 1 1/2 cups cheddar and sautéed onions to grits. Stir till cheese is melted. Add tomatoes and mix well.
Pour into a greased 13"×9" dish and bake for 40 minutes.
Sprinkle remaining cheese over the casserole for the last 5 minutes of cooking.

In Danna's kitchen, you will find treasures that have helped nourish her family for generations.

Front row from left: Mom's Swann's serving dish, which is holding Granny Campbell's drippings bowl; Danna's green and brown drip dishes; the kitchen knife made by Uncle Jack; Great-Grandma Parker's rolling pin and tea strainer.

Back row from left: Granny Campbell's brown dinner plate; Great-Grandma Parker's serving bowl, and Papa Swann's wooden tool box.

Aunt Janice's Bean Pot

1 can kidney or white beans
1 can pork and beans
1 can pinto beans
1/2 lb. bacon, cut in small pieces
1 lb. ground beef, cooked
1 bell pepper, chopped
1 onion, chopped
1 cup catsup
1/2 cup brown sugar
3 tablespoons white vinegar
1 tablespoon liquid smoke
1 teaspoon salt

Chop bacon in small pieces and fry.
Sauté onion and pepper in 1 tablespoon of the bacon grease.
Cook ground beef, crumbled.
Drain all beans and place in a crockpot.
Add bacon, ground beef, onions and pepper.
Stir in catsup, brown sugar, vinegar, salt, and liquid smoke.
Cook on low several hours.

Cheesy Hash Brown Casserole

2 lbs. hash brown potatoes
1/2 cup onions
10 oz shredded cheddar cheese
8 oz sour cream
1 can cream of chicken soup
(For extra cheesy flavor, use nacho cheese soup, instead.)
1 teaspoon salt
1 stick butter, melted
1 to 2 sleeves Ritz crackers, per your taste

Mix first six ingredients together.
Put in a greased casserole dish.
Crush Ritz crackers and sprinkle on top of the potato mixture.
Pour melted butter over crackers.
Bake at 350° for 1 hour 10 minutes or until bubbly and brown.

RiverWood's Bacon Hash Brown Casserole

32 oz frozen hash browns
16 oz sour cream
8 slices bacon, cooked and crumbled
1 oz package ranch dressing mix
2 cups extra sharp shredded cheddar cheese, divided

Preheat oven to 350°.
Combine hash browns, sour cream, bacon, ranch mix, and 1 cup of cheddar.
Mix well.
Spread into a greased baking dish and cover with foil.
Cook for 45 minutes.
Remove foil and sprinkle remaining 1 cup of cheddar over top.
Bake 12-15 minutes or until cheese is bubbly.

Moma Holt made many crocheted doilies. She memorized the patterns as a young lady and created so many through the years. This one graces the wall in our home and is a family treasure.

One Alabama Family's Culinary Heritage and Adventures

Part 5

The Marvelous Moma Holt

What can I say about Moma (this is how she spelled it; therefore, this is how I spell it) Holt? She was a marvel to me. When I married into David's family thirty-eight years ago, she took me in as a grandchild even though she had a multitude of grandchildren already, and I had plenty of grandmothers. She had around 22 grandchildren so what's another one? I never felt like a granddaughter in-law, always like a granddaughter. She had an amazing gift of acceptance and warmly welcomed others into her family circle with joy.

Now that's not to say that things were always perfect in her life. Moma Holt had many trials and tribulations just like we all do. She birthed eleven children and raised twelve and loved them all dearly. That in itself is a feat to contend with. Heavenly days, can you imagine raising twelve children! Can you imagine how much food she cooked on a daily basis? And the laundry...yikes!

One Thanksgiving back in the 1950s, when she had all the children at home, she told her husband, "Now Pop, go down to the store and get the biggest turkey you can find."

She had a lot of mouths to feed, you know. Well, he did. Pop Holt bought the absolute largest turkey in the county! That thing weighed in between 35 and 40 pounds-depending on who is telling the story.

Well, it just took her breath away to look at it. My heavens, that bird was big! It was so big that there wasn't one pan in her kitchen that would hold it. It was too big for any of her pans, and she had large pans because she fed her large family three meals a day. Well, now what was she to do? So, she sent Pop back to the store to buy a something large enough to cook the bird in. He came back with a bath tub! You know, those white porcelain baby bath tubs that had the red rim around the edge? Yep, that's what she cooked her turkey in on that particular Thanksgiving.

When one of her granddaughters had her senior pictures made to commemorate her graduation, Moma Holt liked them so much that she decided to have her senior pictures taken! And she did.

But, after solving that dilemma, she soon realized they had another situation to contend with. It was so big it wouldn't fit in their oven! The door wouldn't close. Well, not to be undone, but they had to figure that one out. And she and Pop did. She was gifted with a big supply of good ol' common sense which came in handy considering how many kids she was raising. She concocted a set-up where half the turkey was in the oven and the other half was sticking out the door. Then she closed the oven door as far as it would go and propped the door up with a kitchen chair. But that turkey was never gonna* get done with the door half open. What to do? Pop Holt had many talents so he concocted a covering of some sort to hold in the heat, and it went all the way around the oven opening. To cook the bird, Moma Holt rotated it continuously throughout the cooking

* Southern vernacular, page 139

time so that the entire ginormous bird was finally roasted and ready for Thanksgiving dinner. She told me that rotating that turkey all day liked to worked her to death.

Now that was a whole lot of turkey. And the whole family relished it the first day. And the second day, too, for every meal. Moma Holt made turkey hash, turkey salad, and turkey sandwiches among other turkey dishes. She was gifted with stretching the family budget and keeping the food as tasty as she could for her family.

In later years, Moma Holt married Simon Tidwell and they spent the rest of their years enjoying one another on the farm.

But on the fourth day, Pop Holt said, "Ruby, how much of that turkey do you have left?"

She said, "Still got enough for a few more meals."

Well now, keep in mind, her family was not used to having leftovers at all because it just didn't happen with that many mouths to feed. It was at that point that Pop Holt decided he had taken his last bite of turkey for the year.

He said, "Throw it out, give it away, go bury it or something! I don't want to taste another bite of turkey till next Thanksgiving!"

And so, they did. And it is now a treasured family story that's been told and passed down through the family since the 1950s. But, a favorite family recipe came from it called Turkey Hash.

Now Moma Holt crocheted, quilted, prayed, tended her flowers, and cooked throughout her entire life. Everything she made, she did at a rapid pace because of raising all those kids. Yes, she got things done in a hurry. And if something turned out a little off and wasn't quite perfect, she would laugh and say, "Let's just put a little rick-rack on it. It'll be fine."

Now, rick-rack is ornamental sewing trim in a zigzag pattern used for decoration. So if someone at the family gathering showed up with a new article made by Moma Holt and it had an odd piece of zigzag trim on it, we would all laugh and say, "Just put a little rack-rack on it!" And, looking back, that just let us know not to take life so seriously all the time...if things are not perfect, just put a little rick-rack on it! Everything's gonna* be alright!

Moma Holt loved life, but there were times when life dealt her serious blows that would have defeated a lesser person. She lost her husband and her youngest daughter within three weeks of each other. What got her through it? Many prayers of her loved ones and a strong faith in God. She lived close to the Lord and was always talking things over with Him.

While our children were small, she lived next to us on our family farm. This allowed for much visiting and laughing. That is how I came to know her recipes and her faith. She would tell me stories of how God had answered her prayers through the years, and I would listen and learn from a woman who had been through so many difficult situations in her life but still managed to hang on to her joy.

There are so many stories she told of answered prayers, but I'll just leave you with a few. Early in 1970, long hair was "in" for men. Their son Hayden was a teenager and just wouldn't get his hair cut. It was getting so long and shaggy in Moma Holt's eyes, and she told him over and over that she wanted it cut. Well, he wouldn't do it. Then, she decided to talk it over with God. She let Him in on her concerns. And you know what? Hayden was working on a car one day right after she prayed, and his long hair caught on fire! Yes, it did! Caught.. on... fire!

Well now, that got his attention. He got it put out pretty quick then ran inside the house and said, "You been praying, ain't you, Momma? My hairs done caught on fire. Look at it! It's a mess now. I'm going to the barber shop to get a haircut!"

Moma Holt laughed and looked to heaven and said, "Thank you, Jesus!"

Forever after that, the family consensus was: you might as well do what Moma Holt asked you to do because she might pray about it. And if she does, then you're gonna end up doing it anyway —because the Good Lord was on her side!

Moma Holt had such faith, and she loved her flowers that she tended to in her yard. One day, she was praying to the Lord while admiring the beautiful flowers. And she told Him that she needed a petunia plant right there, and she touched the soil where she wanted it. And the Good Lord sent her a beautiful white petunia...right there!

Moma Holt was a brilliant illustration of a strong Southern woman who overcame life's obstacles and trials with lots of prayer, tenacity, common sense and a just dab of sparkling joy...along with a little bit of rick-rack!

Moma Holt's Turkey Hash

As told to Danna Standridge

Onion, chopped
Butter
Potatoes, peeled and cut small
Turkey, chopped
Turkey broth
Salt to taste

Melt the butter in the skillet or Dutch oven on top of the stove.
Add the chopped onion and cook till soft.
Add potatoes, chopped turkey, and turkey broth.
Bring to a boil for a few minutes then turn to simmer till all is done.

Danna cooking a 26 pound turkey.

"With God as My Witness" ...

The year was 1951, and times were tough. Many layoffs were happening and people were scrambling to find work so they could feed their families. Moma and Pop Holt had a house full of children in 1951, and it was a job— make that two jobs- to feed them all. Pop Holt worked hard to provide for the family as a coal miner while Moma Holt worked hard at home taking care of the whole bunch. Remember, they had eleven children and raised twelve. There was always a gang around their dining table. And it wasn't unusual to have some of the uncles and cousins there to eat as well.

The little Holt girls. Front row from left: Violet, Sandra and Patty. Back row: Phyllis

Violet and Patty were the poke salat pickers.

Now as a coal miner, things were generally bought at the Commissary which was controlled by the mining company. So, miners worked and got their paycheck and the money was taken out for what they owed the commissary. Well...the work load started to lighten up which meant less hours to work which meant less money coming in to the household. And, it got so bad that when the payday rolled around and the checks came in, there was no money to be had because it was all used to pay the commissary.

But Pop Holt wasn't the regular coal miner. He wouldn't have his family living in the coal camp. No, sir. He wanted his children to have a farm life so he bought a farm and had them growing up in the clean fresh air.

It was along this time that Pop Holt got laid off at the coal mine along with many others. He and his brother Everett and his cousin Newt and his oldest son, Paul, who was married at the time, sat around that kitchen table and said, "Boy if we just had a fifty-cent piece to hold in our hand, wouldn't that be something!"

Times were so lean. Can you imagine just wanting to hold a fifty-cent piece? Their pockets were empty. The word on the street was that Ford Motor Company was hiring. So, off the men went to Michigan to seek a good-paying job.

As I said before, Pop Holt did things differently by raising his children on a farm away from the coal camp. While he used the commissary when necessary, he generally traded with a local general store. So, before he traveled to Michigan, he made arrangements with the storekeeper to give them a line of credit until he could work a few weeks and come back and pay his bill. The two men came to an understanding, and it was agreed upon. So, Pop could leave his family to go find get a job knowing that they would be in good shape until he returned.

Pop was gone, and after groceries got thin, Moma Holt went to the store to stock up. When she got ready to check out, the store keeper told her he had changed his mind and would not be giving her any credit at all. He said it wasn't good for business. So, she went home empty-handed knowing she had a bunch of mouths to feed. There would be no groceries bought until Pop returned.

Well, Michigan is a long way, and the family was happy to find out that Pop got the job! As companies do, they held back his check for few weeks, so there would be no money for groceries for at least three weeks!

Now Moma Holt was glad to hear that he had got the job! But, she didn't want him worrying about the family, so she didn't tell him what happened at the store. She didn't tell him at all. She told him everything was just fine, and then she started working out a plan to keep them all fed until he could get home.

"If we ever make it through this, WE ARE NEVER GOING TO EAT POKE SALAT AGAIN FOR THE REST OF OUR LIFE!

Fortuitously, Moma Holt raised a garden and canned food every year. So, she surveyed the situation and realized she had to stretch that out as far as it would go. But even with her best planning, it was going to be lean.

And then, she remembered how her family loved poke salat. It was one of their favorite dishes! And, it just happened to be springtime when poke salat was at its finest. Things were going to be alright! She would cook them poke salat!

As a mother and manager of such a large clan, Moma Holt gave all of them chores to do on a daily basis. Now little Patty, aged nine, and her big sister Violet, aged eleven, got the chore of picking the poke salat every day! Every day, go find some more poke salat for their family. And then they had to eat it.

Moma Holt still cooked them three meals a day, but one of them was poke salat. The first week, it was okay because, after all, it was a favorite dish of the family. By the second week, Patty and Violet were tired of picking poke salat every day, and the family didn't really want to eat it anymore. But by the third week, it was no longer a family favorite. As a matter of fact, Patty and Violet were sick of picking it and only ate a bite of it to fend off the hunger if they had to.

They did make it through that tough time, and after weeks of being away from his family and working so hard, Pop got home with his first paycheck from Ford Motor Company in his pocket. It was "a sight for sore eyes" for him to see his family. What should have been a celebration turned out differently when Pop found out what had happened. He was furious that the storekeeper had gone back on his word, but proud of how Moma Holt and the family had pulled together to make it through a tough time.

And now, while the family is thankful that poke salat saved them that spring, it was during that third week of picking and eating poke salat that little Patty and Violet vowed to one another, "If we ever make it through this, WE ARE NEVER GOING TO EAT POKE SALAT AGAIN FOR THE REST OF OUR LIFE!

And they haven't.

A snowy day on the Standridge family farm.

Photo by Hayden Shirley

Southerners and Snow: A Delicious Phenomenon

It doesn't snow much in the South. We don't get to enjoy it as often as our Northern cousins do, but we do look forward to snow. We buy our milk and bread to get prepared if the weatherman even mentions the "S" word. We get out of school and get to enjoy the peace and quiet of no traffic on the roads and the beauty of our Southern terrain covered in beautiful white fluff. And it usually melts away by the afternoon so we feel like it is a gift from God to allow us time off to enjoy His creation in a calming way.

Nope, it doesn't snow much in the South, but let me tell you, when we do get a few inches of snow, we make ice cream out of it! Yep, I'm not kidding, we make snow cream as we call it! For generations in my family we have turned snow into a dessert. It's just what you do on a snowy morning after you get tired of throwing snowballs at each other. My great-grandmothers, my grandmothers, my mother, me, and my daughter have all carried on this Southern tradition, and if you have never had snow cream, give it a try! It's an Alabama tradition in our family.

Some of my earliest memories are playing in the snow with my twin sister, my older sister, and my sweet little baby brother. Mom would bundle us up, and off into the snowy world we would go. Running, slipping, rolling, throwing snow balls, and making snowmen were part of our snowy mornings. And when our noses got too cold, in we would go to warm up and eat some of Momma's snow cream.

You see, while we were playing in the snow, our momma sent Daddy on the errand of gathering clean, fresh snow with no animal tracks or debris in it. The optimal place to gather clean snow was the top of the automobiles and the top of the slide of our swing set. Mom sent Dad on the mission with a big bowl and a big spoon. When I had a family of my own, I sent my husband on the snow gathering mission as I bundled up the children for a fun romp in the snow.

And, in case you decide to try it, let me give you a few important hints. Don't scoop to the bottom level of snow on the automobile, leave a half inch of snow behind so as not to collect any dirt. And, heaven forbid, never, ever, ever collect yellow snow!! Just trust me on that one.

The March 1993 Blizzard which covered the entire state of Alabama. From left are the Standridge children, Caleb, Lonna, and Joshua.

The little Swann girls, from left Dinah, Suzanne, and Danna.

Snow Cream!

By Danna Standridge

1 large bowl of fresh snow (2-3 gallons)
2 cups sugar
2 cups milk (heavy cream or evaporated milk may be substituted)
2 teaspoons vanilla

Dissolve sugar in milk. Add vanilla. Taste it. Add more sugar, milk, and vanilla as needed to the mixture to get a strong vanilla ice cream taste. Stir in fresh snow with a large spoon. Add snow a little at a time for best results. When is looks like homemade ice cream, it's ready. Serve immediately.

The Standridge Family

David, Danna, Lonna, Caleb, Joshua
(and Hooch, Maggie and Big Ben)

Danna enjoying time in the kitchen with her granddaughter Sydney Standridge.

Desserts

CAKES

Smooth and Creamy Frosting

1 small instant pudding, your choice on flavor
¼ cup confectioners sugar
1 cup cold milk
1 8 oz Cool Whip

Combine pudding mix, sugar, and milk in small bowl.
Beat slowly at lowest speed until well-blended, about 1 minute.
Fold in whipped topping.
Makes 4 cups of icing, enough for 2 9-inch layers.
Store frosted cake in refrigerator.

Cherry Dump Cake

1 can cherry pie filling, 21 oz
1 can crushed pineapple, 20 oz undrained
yellow cake mix
coconut
pecans
2 sticks butter

Grease a 13″×9″ inch pan.
Pour in cherry pie filling.
Spread drained pineapple on top.
Sprinkle dry cake mix on top.
Sprinkle on coconut and pecans.
Melt butter and pour over the mixture.
Bake at 350° for 1 hour.

The Marvelous Mandarin Orange Cake

Cake Ingredients:
1 yellow butter cake mix
4 eggs
¾ cup cooking oil
1 11 oz can Mandarin oranges

Cake Directions:
Mix cake mix, eggs, and cooking oil.
Add Mandarin oranges, juice and all.
Mix by hand to prevent mashing the oranges.
Pour into 3 greased and floured pans.
Bake at 350° for 18-20 minutes.

Frosting Ingredients:
1 20 oz can crushed pineapple, drained
1 small instant vanilla pudding
1 12 oz Cool Whip

Frosting Directions:
Mix drained crushed pineapple with pudding mix and Cool Whip and ice cake.

Glenda Swann's Red Velvet Cake

Cake Ingredients:
1/2 cup solid Crisco shortening
1 1/2 cups sugar
2 eggs
2 1/2 cups plain flour
1 teaspoon soda
1 teaspoon salt
1 cup buttermilk
2 oz red food coloring
1 teaspoon vanilla
1 teaspoon vinegar
2 teaspoons cocoa

Cake Directions:
Cream Crisco and sugar.
Add eggs and mix.
Sift together flour, soda, salt, and cocoa.
Add to the Crisco mixture alternating with the buttermilk.
Mix food coloring, vanilla, vinegar and add to the main mixture.
Pour in floured and greased cake pans.
Bake in a preheated oven at 350° for 30 minutes.

Frosting Ingredients:
1 1/2 cups milk
6 tablespoons plain flour
1 1/2 cups sugar
pinch salt
1 1/2 teaspoons vanilla
1 cup solid Crisco shortening
1 stick butter, room temperature

Frosting Directions:
Stir flour into milk in a saucepan over medium heat till thick like pudding, stir constantly.
Put in the refrigerator until it gets cold.
Mix in 1 1/2 cups sugar, salt, vanilla and stir. It will be gooey.
Beat together the Crisco and butter. Add to the flour mixture.
Beat at high speed for 8-10 minutes till it looks like whipped cream.
Frost cake.

No Peeking Coconut Cake

1 box white cake mix
1 small package vanilla instant pudding
2 cups sugar
1 8 oz sour cream
12 oz fresh or frozen coconut
1 12 oz Cool Whip

Combine pudding mix with cake mix and prepare according to the directions on the cake mix.
Prepare two cake pans; grease and flour.
Bake cake according to package directions.
While baking, mix the sour cream, sugar, and coconut and let stand while cake is cooling.
Slice each layer to make a total of four layers.
Spread each cake layer with the coconut mixture and top with Cool Whip. Repeat with remaining layers, stacking them. Do not frost the sides. Place cake in a sealed container and store in the refrigerator for three days before serving.
No Peeking!

Southern Punch Bowl Cake

1 yellow cake mix prepared in 2 layer pans according to directions, cooled, and cut into squares
2 large instant French vanilla pudding, prepared according to directions
2 cans cherry pie filling
20 oz crushed pineapple, drained
coconut and pecan, optional
2 8 oz Cool Whips
maraschino cherries

Layer 1—place 1/2 of the cake cubes in punch bowl
Layer 2—Spread 1/2 of drained pineapple over cake
Layer 3—Spread 1/2 pudding
Layer 4—spread 1/2 whipped cream
Layer 5—Spread 1/2 cherry pie filling
Repeat layers and end with a beautiful layer of Cool Whip topped with coconut and pecans if you wish.

Ma-Maw McKee's Chocolate Cake

Cake Ingredients:
2 cups sugar
1 cup milk
3/4 cup Crisco
3 eggs
3 tablespoons vanilla
2 1/2 cups self-rising flour

Cake Directions:
Cream sugar, milk, and Crisco.
Beat eggs one at a time and add to creamed mixture.
Add the flour a little at a time mixing well after each addition.
Stir in the vanilla.
Pour cake batter into greased and floured 8 inch cake pans.
Makes 5 thin layers.
Bake at 350° for 20 minutes or until cake tests done.

Icing Ingredients:
1/2 cup butter
3 cups sugar
2/3 cup cocoa
1/4 teaspoon salt
1 1/2 cups milk
2 tablespoons vanilla

Icing Directions:
Melt butter in a large skillet.
Mix sugar, cocoa, and salt together in bowl.
Add melted butter, stir in milk, and stir in vanilla.
Cook over medium-high heat until bubbly.
Do not overcook as the cake layers are thin and the icing shouldn't be too heavy.
Spread icing in between layers and on top of cooled cake.

Apple Cake

Cake Ingredients:
1 1/2 cups vegetable oil
3 cups self-rising flour
1 teaspoon vanilla
1/2 teaspoon salt

1 teaspoon cinnamon
2 cups sugar
3 cups diced apples
2 eggs

Cake Directions:
In a mixing bowl blend all the ingredients. The mixture will be thick.
Bake in a 9"×13" greased pan at 300° for 1 1/2 hours.

Icing Ingredients:
3/4 cup brown sugar
1/2 stick butter
1/4 cup sweetened condensed milk
1 teaspoon vanilla

Icing Directions:
Bring all ingredients to a boil and pour over cake

German Chocolate Upside-Down Cake

1 cup coconut
1 cup chopped pecans
1 2-layer German Chocolate cake mix
1/3 cup melted butter
8 oz cream cheese
1 box confectioner's sugar

Sprinkle coconut and pecans into buttered 9"×13" dish.
Prepare cake mix as directed on package.
Spread evenly in prepared pan.
Blend butter, cream cheese, and confectioners sugar in mixer.
Spread over batter.
Bake at 350° for 35-45 minutes or until cake tests done.

Strawberry Layer Cake

Cake Ingredients:
1 box white cake mix
1 small strawberry Jell-O
1 cup fresh strawberries*
2/3 cup oil
4 whole eggs

Cake Directions:
Mix cake mix, Jell-O, oil, and eggs. Beat for 3 minutes.
Add strawberries and beat 1 minute.
Pour batter into 3 greased cake pans and bake in a 350° oven for 25 minutes.
Cool completely and frost with strawberry icing.

Icing Ingredients:
1 stick butter
1 box powdered sugar
1/2 cup fresh strawberries

Icing Directions:
Cream butter and 1 cup powdered sugar.
Gradually add strawberries and the rest of the powdered sugar.

*If using frozen strawberries, drain off most of the juice.

David and Danna

Cousin Donna's Italian Cream Cake

Cake Ingredients:
2 cups sugar
1 stick butter, room temperature
1/2 cup shortening
5 eggs, separated
2 cups plain flour
1 teaspoon baking soda
1 cup buttermilk
1 teaspoon vanilla
1 4 oz can coconut
1 cup chopped pecans

Cake Directions:
Beat egg whites until stiff and set aside.
Cream butter and shortening, add sugar gradually.
Add egg yolks one at a time.
Add baking soda to flour.
Alternate adding flour and buttermilk into mixture.
Add vanilla, coconut, and pecans.
Fold in stiffly beaten egg whites.
Pour into 3 greased and floured cake pans. Bake at 350° for 25 minutes

Icing Ingredients:
8 oz cream cheese, room temperature
1/4 cup butter, softened
1 box powdered sugar
1 teaspoon vanilla
1 cup chopped pecans

Icing Directions:
Mix all ingredients together adding the nuts last.
Frost cake.

In my opinion, for the best 3 layer cake, make 1 1/2 batches of this recipe.

Old Fashioned Carrot Cake

Cake Ingredients:
3 cups carrots, grated
2 cups sugar
2 cups all purpose flour
1 1/4 teaspoon cinnamon
2 teaspoons baking soda
1 teaspoon baking powder
1/2 teaspoon salt
1 1/4 cups oil
4 eggs
1 teaspoon vanilla
8 oz crushed pineapple, drained

Cake Directions:
Combine the first seven ingredients.
Beat your eggs, add vanilla and oil, and gradually mix into the dry ingredients.
Stir in drained pineapple.
Pour batter into three greased and floured cake pans.
Bake at 350° for 30 minutes.

Frosting Ingredients:
8 oz cream cheese, softened
16 oz powdered sugar
1/2 cup butter, softened
1 teaspoon vanilla
1 cup chopped pecans

Frosting Directions:
Cream butter, sugar, cream cheese, and vanilla.
Stir in pecans.
Frost top of cake and in between the layers.

Spread the cream cheese frosting between the cake layers and on the top while the cake is still warm.
Don't frost the sides.

Apple Sauce Cake

1/2 cup butter
1 cup sugar
1 egg
1 cup dates, finely chopped
1 cup applesauce
1 cup nuts, chopped fine
1 cup raisins, chopped
1 teaspoon cinnamon
1/2 teaspoon cloves
1 teaspoon vanilla
1 3/4 cups flour
1 teaspoon baking soda

Cream butter and sugar, add egg till well-beaten.
Add the vanilla and the remainder of the ingredients.
Pour into a well-buttered bread pan.
Bake at 350° for one hour.

Rita's Cream Cheese Pound Cake

1 1/2 cups butter
8 oz cream cheese, softened
3 cups sugar
6 eggs
3 cups all-purpose flour
1 1/2 teaspoons vanilla

Cream butter and cream cheese, add sugar mixing well.
Add eggs one at a time, beating after each addition.
Add flavoring.
Add flour gradually. Mix well.
Bake in a greased and floured Bundt pan at 325° for 1 1/2 hours.

Hummingbird Cake

Cake Ingredients:
3 cups plain flour
1 teaspoon baking soda
1 teaspoon salt
3 eggs, beaten
1 1/2 cup canola oil
3 oz can crushed pineapples
2 cups chopped bananas
2 cups sugar
1 teaspoon cinnamon
1 1/2 teaspoons vanilla
1 cup chopped pecans

Cake Directions:
Combine soda, flour, cinnamon, sugar, and salt together. Add eggs and oil stirring until all dry ingredients are moistened. Do not beat.
Stir in vanilla, pineapple, pecans, and bananas.
Spoon batter into three greased and floured pans.
Bake at 350° for 25-30 minutes.
Cool in pans for 10 minutes and then cool completely and frost with cream cheese frosting.

Cream Cheese Frosting Ingredients:
8 oz cream cheese, softened
1 box confectioners' sugar
1 stick butter, soft
1 teaspoon vanilla
1/4 cup pecans, toasted

Frosting Directions:
Cream together cream cheese and butter.
Add sugar and vanilla. Mix until smooth. Frost cake.
Sprinkle top of cake with toasted pecans.

Ms. Charlcey's Best Sweet Potato Pie

1 cup cooked sweet potatoes
2 cups sugar
3 eggs
1 stick butter
2/3 cup buttermilk
1 teaspoon nutmeg
1 teaspoon vanilla
2 slightly cooked pie shells

Mix all the ingredients together and pour into pie shells.
The consistency is like water.
Sprinkle additional nutmeg on top of pie.
Bake at 350° approximately one hour.
Pie will be firm to the touch when ready.

Family treasures: recipes from Great-Aunt Lillian Parker, wooden dough bowl from Great-Granny Davidson, wooden spatula from Nanny Swann, biscuit cutters from Great-Grandma Thomas, and an old photo of Great-Grandma and Grandpa Thomas.

Granny Dera's Old Fashioned Chocolate Pie

Pie Ingredients:
1 1/2 cups sugar
4 tablespoons corn starch
3 tablespoons cocoa
2 cups milk
3 egg yolks
1 teaspoon vanilla
1 baked pie crust

Meringue Ingredients:
3 egg whites
2 tablespoons sugar
1 teaspoon cream of tartar

Pie Directions:
Mix sugar, corn starch, and cocoa together. Add milk.
Add beaten egg yolks to pie mixture.
Cook in top of double boiler until thickened. Stir in vanilla.
Pour into baked pie shell.

Meringue Directions:
Beat egg whites until stiff. Add sugar and beat well.
Add cream of tartar. Pile meringue on top of pie filling.
Bake at 350° until brown.

Mini Cheesecakes

12 vanilla wafers
2 8 oz cream cheese, softened
Foil cupcake liners
1/2 cup sugar
1 teaspoon vanilla
2 eggs

Toppings:
your choice of fruit, preserves, or chocolate

Place cupcake liners in muffin tin.
Place 1 vanilla wafer in each liner.
Mix cream cheese, vanilla, and sugar on medium speed until well-blended.
Add eggs and mix well.
Pour over wafers filling 3/4 full.
Bake 25 minutes in a preheated 325° oven.
Remove from pan when cool.
Add your favorite toppings.
Store in the refrigerator.

Barbara's Buttermilk Pie

1/2 teaspoon vanilla
1/2 cup coconut
1/2 cup buttermilk
1/2 cup pecans
1 1/4 cups sugar
3 eggs
1/4 cup butter
1 tablespoon flour
1 pie crust

Mix all ingredients together.
Pour into pie crust.
Bake at 350° for 45 minutes.

Lillian's Coconut Cream Pie

2 eggs, separated
1/2 cup sugar
5 tablespoons flour
1 cup evaporated milk
1 cup water
1 cup coconut
pinch salt
1 teaspoon vanilla
4 tablespoons butter
1 pie shell
1/4 cup sugar
1/4 teaspoon cream of tartar

Separate your eggs.
Blend egg yolks and next six ingredients and cook over medium heat stirring frequently until thick.
Remove from heat and stir in vanilla and butter.
Use the egg whites and remaining ingredients to make meringue.

Fresh Peach Pie

1 9" baked pie crust
1 cup sugar
1 cup water
3 tablespoons cornstarch
juice of one lemon
1/2 stick butter
2 cups fresh peaches
whipped cream

In a saucepan, mix cornstarch with sugar and add water.
Cook over medium heat until it is thick and clear.
Add lemon juice and butter.
Let the glaze cool.
Slice peaches. Stir peaches into cooled glaze.
Pour into pie crust and chill till firm. Top with whipped cream and serve.

Old-Timey Finger Pie

1 pint heavy cream
1 unbaked pie shell
1 cup granulated sugar
2 tablespoons flour
1/2 brown sugar
1/2 teaspoon nutmeg
1/2 teaspoon cinnamon

Pour cream into the pie shell.
Mix the granulated sugar, flour, cinnamon, and nutmeg and sprinkle over the cream.
Tap mixture lightly with finger, do not stir, till the mixture sinks into the cream.
Sprinkle brown sugar on the top and bake at 350° degrees for 45 minutes to 1 hour.
Serve warm.

Old Fashioned Coconut Pies

Makes 2 pies

1 stick butter
2 cups sugar
4 tablespoons flour
6 eggs
2 cups milk
2 teaspoons vanilla
1 can angel flake coconut
2 unbaked pie crusts

In a double boiler, melt butter over hot water.
Add sugar and stir well.
Add flour and blend well.
Add eggs one at a time, beating after each addition.
Add the milk, coconut, and vanilla.
Pour into the two pie crusts and bake at 350° degrees for about 30 minutes or until done.

Best Fruit Cobbler and Pie Crust

Cobbler Ingredients:
4 cups frozen fruit*
1 1/2 cups sugar
3 tablespoons cornstarch
1 stick butter
1 pie crust (directions below)

*Can use apples, peaches, blueberries, blackberries or cherries.
For apples, add some cinnamon and nutmeg.

Cobbler Directions:
Place fruit in a 9"×13" dish. Mix cornstarch and sugar together and sprinkle over the fruit. Dot with butter. Cover with pie crust, cut a vent in top and use an egg wash over top of crust.
Bake at 425° for 30 minutes.

Optional—for a sweet crunch, sprinkle a small amount of sugar over the crust.

Pie Crust Ingredients:
5 cups flour
2 1/2 cups shortening
1/2 teaspoon salt
1 egg
2 teaspoons vinegar

Pie Crust Directions:
Mix dry ingredients and shortening together.
In a measuring cup, beat the egg, then add 2 teaspoons vinegar.
To the egg mixture, add enough water to make 1 full cup. Stir well.
Pour into the flour mixture and mix. Divide into 6 balls. Freeze unused dough.

Granny Campbell's Chocolate Pudding

1 1/2 cups sugar
1/2 cup flour
dash of salt
3/4 cup cocoa
3 eggs, separated
1 large can evaporated milk
2 cups milk
1/4 cup butter
1 teaspoon vanilla

Mix dry ingredients—sugar, flour, salt, cocoa—in top of a double boiler.
Beat egg yolks in a separate bowl and stir in evaporated milk.
Add egg mixture slowly to the dry ingredient smoothing out lumps.
Add 2 cups milk, cooking over simmering water, stirring until it thickens.
Add vanilla and stir in butter.
Place in a buttered dish.

Meringue:
Beat egg whites and 2 tablespoons sugar.
Place on pudding and bake at 350° for 10 minutes.

Old-Fashioned Banana Pudding

Pudding Ingredients:
3 eggs
2 tablespoons corn starch
1 1/2 cups sugar
2 cups milk
1 teaspoon vanilla
Vanilla wafers
3 to 4 bananas
salt

Meringue Ingredients:
3 egg whites
3 tablespoons sugar
1 teaspoon cream of tartar

Pudding Directions:
Mix sugar, salt, and corn starch in saucepan on medium heat.
Add milk and stir in pan to make a paste.
Separate eggs.
Stir yolks well and add a little of the hot mixture.
Stir and return to the pan.
Cook a little longer, a minute or two.
Remove from heat and add vanilla.
Layer in a bowl starting with bananas then vanilla wafers,
Put another layer of bananas and vanilla wafers.
Pour cooled custard over the vanilla wafers. You may want to poke the filling through the wafers making sure it goes to the bottom.

Meringue Directions:
Beat egg whites with sugar until stiff.
Add cream of tartar.
Put meringue on top of pudding.
Bake until meringue is brown.

Blueberry Cobbler

20 oz crushed pineapple, do not drain
3 cups blueberries
3/4 cup sugar sprinkled over berries
1 yellow cake mix
1 stick butter, melted
1/4 cup sugar, sprinkled over mix
1/2 cup chopped pecans

Butter a 9"×13" dish.
Layer the ingredients as listed above. Do not stir.
Bake for 45 minutes at 350°.

Tart Apple Crisp

6 tart apples, peeled and cut into eighths
1 cup granulated sugar
1 stick butter
1/2 cup brown sugar
1 cup flour
1/2 teaspoon cinnamon

Place apples into a casserole dish. Cover with granulated sugar and sprinkle with cinnamon.
Blend together butter, brown sugar, and flour till it resembles meal.
Spread over apples.
Bake at 350° degrees for one hour.

EVERYTHING ELSE:

From Cookies to Brownies to Candy to Muffins

Granny's Egg Custard

1 cup sugar
1 cup scalded milk
3 beaten eggs
1 teaspoon vanilla
1 pie crust
1/8 teaspoon salt
nutmeg (to taste)

Mix sugar, beaten eggs, salt, and vanilla.
Add scalded milk and pour into prepared pie shell.
Sprinkle top with nutmeg.
Bake at 450° for 10 minutes then reduce to 350° for about 30 minutes.
Cook until firm and the pastry is brown.

Mountain Dew Dumplings

2 Granny Smith apples, peeled, cored, cut into 8 slices
2 cans crescent rolls
2 sticks butter
cinnamon
1 1/2 cups sugar
1 teaspoon vanilla
8 oz Mountain Dew

Wrap apple slices in crescent roll dough. Place in buttered 9"×13" dish.
Melt butter then add sugar. Stir slightly.
Add vanilla and stir.
Pour over apples. Pour Mountain Dew around the edges of the dough-wrapped apples. Sprinkle with cinnamon.
Cook until golden brown. Is good served with ice cream.

Fruit Pizza

1 roll refrigerated sugar cookie dough
1 (8 oz) cream cheese, softened
1/2 cup powdered sugar
Choice of fruit: sliced strawberries, kiwi, peaches, bananas, grapes, etc.
1 cup orange juice
1/2 cup sugar
1 tablespoon corn starch

Pat cookie dough into lightly greased pizza pan.
Bake at 350° for 8-10 minutes. Let cool completely.
Combine cream cheese and powdered sugar, blending well.
Spread over cookie crust.
Arrange fruit over cream cheese.
In a saucepan, combine orange juice, sugar and cornstarch, bring to a boil and cook, stirring often until thickened.
Cool and pour over fruit.
Refrigerate till time to serve.

Some of Danna's very favorite measuring cups.

Four Layer Delight

1 cup flour
1 stick butter, melted
1/2 cup chopped pecans
1 8 oz cream cheese, softened
1 cup powdered sugar
1 12 oz Cool Whip, divided
2 large boxes chocolate or lemon instant pudding
5 cups milk

Combine flour, butter, and pecans. Pat into 9”×13” pan.
Bake in preheated oven at 350° for 20 minutes till golden brown.
Cool completely.
In bowl, cream together the sugar and cream cheese.
Fold in 1 cup Cool Whip.
Spread over cooled crust.
In another bowl, combine pudding mix and milk.
Beat at low speed for 2 minutes.
Pour over cream cheese mixture.
Spread remaining Cool Whip and refrigerate.

No Bake Chocolate Oatmeal Cookies

2 cups sugar
1/2 cup evaporated milk
1 stick butter
pinch of salt
4 tablespoons cocoa
1 cup peanut butter
3 cups oatmeal

Combine sugar, milk, butter, salt, and cocoa in a heavy saucepan.
Bring to a boil slowly.
Cook 1 minute and remove from heat.
Add peanut butter and oatmeal.
Mix well and drop by spoonfuls onto buttered foil.
Cool and enjoy.

Granny's Divinity

2 1/2 cups sugar
1/2 cup corn syrup
1/8 teaspoon salt
2/3 cup water
2 egg whites
1 1/2 cups chopped nuts
1 teaspoon vanilla

Combine sugar, corn syrup, salt, and water in a saucepan.
Cook to the softball stage, about 240°.
Take out 1/2 cup of the syrup mixture and set aside.
Cook the remaining syrup mixture to hard ball stage, about 250-260°.
Beat the egg whites to stiff peaks and slowly pour the 1/2 cup of softball stage mixture over them, beating constantly.
Now add remaining hardball syrup, beating constantly.
Add nuts and vanilla and keep beating until mixture is heavy and thick.
Drop by teaspoon onto buttered surface. Must move quickly before candy sets.

Applesauce Raisin Muffins

1 large egg
2 tablespoons vegetable oil
1 1/2 cups unsweetened applesauce
2 cups unbleached white flour
3/4 teaspoon baking soda
2 teaspoons baking powder
1/2 teaspoon nutmeg
1/2 teaspoon cinnamon
3/4 cup raisins
pinch of salt
cream cheese (optional)

Beat together egg, oil, and applesauce.
Add flour, baking soda, baking powder, salt, and spices. Beat well.
Stir in raisins. Spoon batter into oiled and floured muffin pans.
Bake at 375° for 20 to 25 minutes or until firm and browned.
Cool on a wire rack.
Delicious topped with cream cheese.

One Spoon Cocoa Brownies

1 2/3 cups granulated sugar
1 1/2 sticks butter, melted
2 tablespoons water
2 eggs, beaten
2 teaspoons vanilla
1 1/3 cups self-rising flour
3/4 cup cocoa

With a spoon, stir together sugar, butter, and water.
Stir in beaten eggs and vanilla.
Add flour and cocoa and stir until blended.
Spread the thick batter into a greased 9"×13" pan.
Bake at 350° for 18-25 minutes until toothpick inserted in center comes out slightly sticky.
Cool and enjoy!

Donna's Pecan Pie Muffins

1 cup packed brown sugar
1 cup chopped pecans
2 eggs, beaten
1 1/2 cups flour
2/3 cup soft butter

Grease and flour miniature muffin tins.
Combine flour, brown sugar, and pecans.
Crumble with hands until coarse.
In separate bowl, beat butter and eggs.
Stir in dry ingredients until creamy.
Fill tins 2/3 the way full.
Bake at 350° for 15-18 minutes.

Lemon Crescent Rolls

8 oz cream cheese, softened
1/2 cup sugar
1 tablespoon lemon juice
1 roll of crescent rolls

Mix cream cheese, sugar, and lemon juice together.
Spread on crescent rolls.
Roll up as directed on package. Place on a greased baking sheet.
Bake until lightly brown.
Cool on wire racks. (If you don't cool on wire racks, they will get soggy.)

Pecan Tassies

Dough Ingredients:
3/4 stick butter
3 oz cream cheese, softened
1 cup plain flour

Dough Directions:
Mix all together and work dough until smooth.
Roll into 24 balls.
Press with fingers into small muffin tins to form a cup.

Filling Ingredients:
1 egg
1/4 stick butter
3/4 cup brown sugar
1 teaspoon vanilla
1 cup finely chopped pecans

Filling Directions:
Mix all ingredients and drop 1 teaspoon into uncooked shells.
Bake at 350° for 30 minutes.

One Alabama Family's Culinary Heritage and Adventures

Part 6

Our favorite pumpkin pie

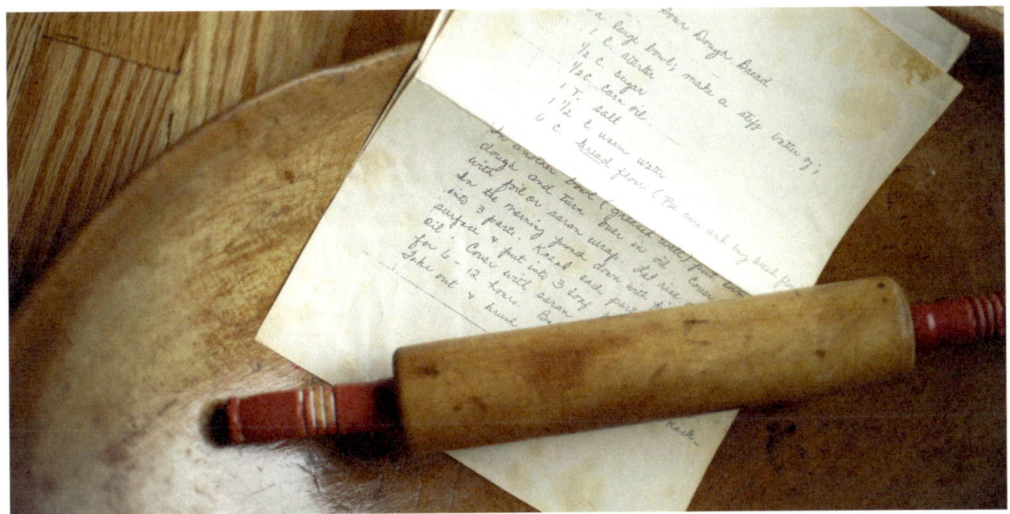

Passing It on with Grandma's Rolling Pin

One branch of my family arrived in the Alabama Territory in 1818. I am so thankful my ancestors realized that Alabama was our family's promised land and stayed to settle in and be a part of what would become the great state of Alabama.

This book has given me a great gift. As I wrote the stories, I was able to look back over the lives and times of my family since Alabama became a state in 1819. What I found in my family is what many of our Alabama families have embedded in their DNA: fortitude, grit, and determination along with a heaping-helping of hospitality.

I found out who we are through our stories and recipes. When my great-grandma Parker passed, I was gifted with her rolling pin. It's just a normal old rolling pin with red handles, but it gives me strength every time I look at it. When my son was shipped off to defend our country, I thought so often on my grandma Parker and the God-fearing strength she needed to cope with her son missing in World War II for eighteen months. I looked at her rolling pin often, and it gave me strength. I said to myself, "If Grandma Parker made it through that, then I can make it through sending my son to Afghanistan."

When thinking of my ancestors and the times they went through, both good and bad, I have hope. Hope that my children and grandchildren will learn where they came from, what our Alabama families have been through, both the triumphs and the hard times. My hope is that this knowledge will propel them into the future and sustain them with the certainty that we are Alabamians and that we will prevail and gain strength as we gather around our tables, love one another, and break bread together.

When I cook with my grandchildren in the kitchen as the flour flies, so do the family stories.

Danna in the kitchen with her granddaughter Leah Dillard. "As the flour flies, so do the family stories."

Danna's Darlings

There is nothing sweeter than passing on our family recipes to our grandchildren. Here are a few of our favorites. Enjoy!

Our Favorite Fresh Strawberry Pound Cake

Danna with her grandson J. D. Dillard

By James David Dillard and Danna Standridge

2 sticks butter, softened
2 cups granulated sugar
3 large eggs
2 tablespoons lemon juice, divided
Zest of 1 lemon
2 1/2 cups all-purpose flour, divided (if using self-rising, omit the salt)
1/2 teaspoon baking soda
1/2 teaspoon salt
8 oz plain or vanilla yogurt
12 oz fresh strawberries, washed and diced
1 cup powdered sugar

Preheat oven to 375°.
Grease and flour a Bundt pan.
Sift together 2 1/4 cups of flour with baking soda and salt.
Mix in lemon zest and set aside.
With mixer in mixing bowl, cream the butter and granulated sugar.
Beat in eggs one at a time.
Stir in 1 tablespoon lemon juice.
Alternate adding the four mixture and the yogurt until just incorporated.
Toss the diced strawberries with the remaining 1/4 cup of flour and stir into batter.
Pour into Bundt pan.
Reduce temperature to 325°.
Bake for 60 minutes or until a toothpick comes out clean.
Cool for 20 minutes in the pan.
Turn out to a wire rack and cool completely.
Whisk together 2 tablespoons lemon juice with the powdered sugar.
Drizzle over top of cake.

Our Favorite Pumpkin Pie

Danna in the kitchen with her granddaughter. Leah is using her great-great-great Grandmother Parker's rolling pen.

By Leah Dillard and Danna Standridge

1 15 oz can of pumpkin
1 14 oz can sweetened condensed milk
2 large eggs
1 teaspoon cinnamon
1/2 teaspoon ground ginger
1/2 teaspoon salt
1 9-inch unbaked pie shell

Preheat oven to 425°.
Combine pumpkin, condensed milk, eggs, spices, and salt until smooth.
Pour into crust.
Bake 15 minutes.
Reduce oven temperature to 350° and continuing baking 35 to 40 minutes or until knife comes out clean inserted 1 inch from the crust.

Our Favorite Cornbread

Danna and her grandson Jasper in the library with her vintage cookbook collection.

By Jasper Standridge and Danna Standridge

3 tablespoons shortening
3/4 cup self-rising cornmeal
1/4 cup self-rising flour
1 egg
3/4 cup buttermilk
1 tablespoon white vinegar
2 small cast iron skillets (6 inch diameter)

Preheat oven to 475°.
Divided the shortening into the small skillets and place in oven to melt during preheating.
Mix flour, meal, egg, buttermilk, and vinegar.
Stir to combine.
Add melted shortening.
The batter needs to be thin for the best cornbread. So add water if needed.
Pour into skillets.
Bake for 10 minutes.
Serves four.

Our Favorite Mashed Potatoes

By Wyatt Dillard and Danna Standridge

5 pounds potatoes, Yukon Gold or russets
2 or 3 sticks butter per your tastes
1 cup heavy cream
milk, enough to thin out to creamy consistency
1 cup sour cream
salt and pepper (to taste)

Wash, peel, and chop potatoes into similar size pieces.
Place in large pan.
Put enough water into pan to cover potatoes by 1 inch.
Add 1/2 tablespoon salt to water
Bring to a boil, then simmer till potatoes are done or until fork tender.
Drain water from pan.
Mash with a potato masher.
Add 1 stick butter, heavy cream, sour cream, salt and pepper.
Continue mashing with a potato masher.
Add milk in small increments and stir until to correct consistency.
Taste often and add butter, salt, and pepper as needed to suit your tastes.

Danna and grandson Wyatt Dillard

Our Favorite Scrambled Eggs

By Sydney Standridge and Danna Standridge

10 large eggs
1/4 stick butter
1/2 cup water
salt and pepper (to taste)

Crack eggs into mixing bowl.
Poke the egg yolks with a fork to break them.
Add water.
Whisk together.
Add salt and pepper.
Melt butter in skillet over medium heat.
Pour eggs in skillet.
Stir gently and often to keep from sticking.
When eggs are firm pour into serving plate and enjoy.

Danna and granddaughter Sydney Standridge

The little Swann girls with Oak Grove Church, from left Suzanne, Dinah, and Danna.

What Did You Say?
Understanding Our Southern Vernacular

Vernacular is how we talk in our everyday language. (And, just so you know, yes, we have been taught proper English, and we polish it off and use it in polite company.) Alabamians have been raised with a wonderful variety of sayings and Southernisms. As one of my "transplanted from the North" college professors stated, "This is the only place I have ever been where people draw you a picture with their language."

When you hear us spout off a Southern saying, how do you know what it means if you're not from here? Here ya go—a Southern vernacular dictionary.

Not blood-kin means someone who is not related to you by genetics. You do not share common genes or common ancestors. It could refer to a friend, a stranger, or someone who married into the family. It could be used for informational purposes or used as an insult. Example, "He's a nice guy and all, but he's not blood-kin. Meaning "my family is smart enough not to do something this stupid, but thankfully he/she is not part of my genetic heritage, therefore, ..." Well, you get the idea.

And, if one of your blood-kin or, heaven forbid, you, does do something stupid, let the teasing begin. Someone is going to remind your family that, "That's your blood right there. Your blood-kin."

This is a favorite at our family table. If the story-telling gets a little too colorful, you got to pay up!

Heaven forbid—we hope the Good Lord is not going to let that happen.

Smack-dab—exactly

Bushed—exhausted

Do it or die trying—determined to achieve

Umpteenth time—happened so many times you have lost count

Lord, yes YES!—emphatically

Took a turn—changed

Tumped over—a combination of turned over and dumped out

Fine and dandy—all is well and things are good

Mess of turnip greens—enough to make a big pot of turnip greens for the family. Now, turnip greens shrink down a lot when you cook them, so to get a pot of greens, you have to pick about triple what the pot will hold.

Ol'—sometimes we don't say all the letters in the word, okay? This is our way of saying the word "old."

Gonna—going to. Just another example of us not saying all the letters in a word.

Have your plate helped—means to make your selections to your momma or aunt or granny and get the food on your plate from the vast array of offerings sitting on the table, stove, and all the kitchen counters.

Did you eat yet?—A commonly heard question from many a genteel southern lady when visitors arrive at her door.

Y'all—a shorthand version of "you all"

About the Author

When you talk to Danna, you will find she loves to laugh and is dedicated to her God, her family, her country, and Sweet Home Alabama! And, like her father, she always has a story to tell.

Danna Swann Standridge has family roots that run deep into Alabama's soil. She was born in Blount County to a family who has made their home in Alabama since 1818. She grew up on a cattle farm. She married her high school sweetheart, David Standridge, who also grew up on a farm in Blount County. They are members of Hayden First Baptist Church and are blessed with three children and five grandchildren.

Danna graduated Summa cum laude from Athens State University with a bachelor of science degree in education. She earned a double major in biology and English and received the Outstanding Biology Major Award. She is also a graduate of Wallace State Community College, summa cum laude.

While her children were young, Danna stayed home to raise the family and later went on to teach public school at her alma mater, Hayden High School. She organized many clubs and extracurricular activities. She taught biology, AP biology, anatomy, and English classes. She took biology students to Dauphin Island Sea Lab to study marine biology and ecosystems.

Community service and leadership are important to Danna. While at Hayden High School, she created and implemented a student leadership program. After leaving the classroom, Danna worked with Auburn University through the Alabama Cooperative Extension System in youth leadership and community classes. This enabled her, along with the support of Blount County Superintendent, to develop and implement the Blount County Ambassador Leadership Program in all seven county high schools where students earn community service hours as they serve their school and community.

Danna has served as both president and chaplain for the Alabama Legislative Club, which is composed of the spouses of the state legislators. During her tenure as president, she worked to secure the Alabama Legislative Art Gallery in the state capitol which features artwork from Alabama artists.

As the wife of state representative for District 34, David Standridge, Danna is an advocate for rural Alabama, youth leadership, education, and Southern traditions. David and Danna are honored to work together for the good of the district and the state of Alabama.

Danna loves reading, writing, collecting vintage cookbooks, knitting, fishing, driving her '57 Chevy, and spending time with the family, including her two dogs and a cat. And, of course, she loves to cook.

INDEX

Appetizers

Aunt Jan's Thanksgiving Celery 18
Aunt Virgie Holt's Chili Sauce 20
Dinah's Stuffed Jalapeno Peppers 20
Jalapeno-Pimento Dip 19
Pimento Cheese 20
Salted Pecans 19
Sausage Balls 18

Beverages

Mocha Punch 21
Shirley Swann's Spiced Tea 21

Breads

4 Generations Sour Dough Bread 16
Applesauce Raisin Muffins 129
Biscuits 14
Biscuits, Ugly 27
Cornbread, Gerald's 80
Donna's Pecan Pie Muffin 130
Kim's Mexican Cornbread 14
Our Favorite Cornbread 136
Poppy Seed Bread 15

Cakes

Apple Cake 111
Apple Sauce Cake 115
Cherry Dump Cake 106
Cousin Donna's Italian Cream Cake 113
German Chocolate Upside-Down Cake 111
Glenda Swann's Red Velvet Cake 108
Hummingbird Cake 116
Ma-Maw McKee's Chocolate Cake 110
Marvelous Mandarin Orange Cake 107
Mini Cheesecakes 119
No Peeking Coconut Cake 109
Old Fashioned Carrot Cake 114
Our Favorite Fresh Strawberry Pound Cake 135
Rita's Cream Cheese Pound Cake 115
Sorghum Syrup Skillet Cake 44
Southern Punch Bowl Cake 109
Strawberry Layer Cake 112

Cheese

Cheddar Cheese and Chicken Casserole 53
Cheesy Hash Brown Casserole 93
Easy Bacon and Cheese Quiche 68
Easy Cheesy El Gando 49
Easy Cheesy Enchiladas 62
Macaroni and Cheese 90
Mini Cheesecakes 119
Ms. Vera's Cheesy Corn Casserole 89
Pimento Cheese 20
Rita's Cream Cheese Pound Cake 115

Desserts

Butter Roll Dessert 43
Granny Campbell's Chocolate Pudding 123
Mini Cheesecakes 119
Old-Fashioned Banana Pudding 124
Tart Apple Crisp 125

Eggs

Our Favorite Scrambled Eggs 137

Everything Else

Applesauce Raisin Muffins 129
Donna's Pecan Pie Muffins 130
Four Layer Delight 128
Fruit Pizza 127
Granny's Divinity 129
Granny's Egg Custard 126
Lemon Crescent Rolls 131
Mountain Dew Dumplings 126
No Bake Chocolate Oatmeal Cookies 128
One Spoon Cocoa Brownies 130
Pecan Tassies 131

Fish & Seafood
Beth and Phil's Shrimp Gumbo....71
Betty's Shrimp Chowder....72
David's Oven Fried Fish....72

Gravy
Granny's Brown-Eyed Gravy....7
Moma Holt's Sausage Gravy....33

Icing
Apple Cake Icing....111
Carrot Cake Icing....114
Chocolate Cake Icing....110
German Chocolate Cake Icing....111
Hummingbird Cake Icing....116
Italian Cream Cake Icing....113
Mandarin Orange Cake Icing....107
Red Velvet Cake Icing....108
Smooth and Creamy Frosting....106
Strawberry Cake Icing....112

Meats
BEEF
Beef Tips and Gravy....63
Corned Beef and Cabbage....66
Country Fried Steak and Gravy....64
Easy Cheesy El Gando....49
Easy Cheesy Enchiladas....62
Gran-Gran's Hot Tamales....59
Kim's Sausage Roll....58
Lillian's Hamburger Bean Casserole....64
Moma Holt's Beef Tips and Noodles....66
Moma Holt's Cabbage Rolls....61
Polynesian Steak....58
Quick and Easy Lasagna....60
Southern Hamburger Pie....60
Stuffed Bell Peppers....63
Sunday Best Pot Roast....62
Swiss Steak....65
Tater Tot Casserole....66
CHICKEN
Broccoli and Chicken Casserole....54
Cheddar Cheese and Chicken Casserole....53
Chicken and Dressing, Nanny Swann's....3
Chicken and Dumplings, Nanny Swann's....30
Chicken Casserole....54
Chicken Pie, Yummy....11
Lorene's Skillet-Fried Chicken....52
Mom's Comfort Chicken....53
Southern Parmesan Chicken....52
PORK
Easy Bacon and Cheese Quiche....68
Lorene's One Pot Meal....68
Pork Chop Skillet Dinner....67
Shirley's Saucy Pork Chops....67
TURKEY
I Can't Believe It's Not Beef! Turkey Chili....56
Moma Holt's Turkey Hash....97
Roasted Turkey, Nanny Swann's Best....2
Turkey Meatloaf....57
VENISON
Fabulous RiverWood Venison Tenderloin with Mushroom Cream Sauce....69
Venison Roast....70
Venison Stew with Veggies....40
Venison Stroganoff....70

Pies, savory
Chicken Pie, Yummy....11
Easy Bacon and Cheese Quiche....68

Pies, sweet
Barbara's Buttermilk Pie....119
Best Fruit Cobbler and Pie Crust....122
Blueberry Cobbler....125
Fresh Peach Pie....120
Fried Apple Pies, Shirley's....7
Granny Dera's Old Fashioned Chocolate Pie....118
Lillian's Coconut Cream Pie....120
Ms. Charlcey's Best Sweet Potato Pie....117
Old Fashioned Coconut Pies....121
Old-Timey Finger Pie....121
Our Favorite Pumpkin Pie....136
Sweet Potato Pie, Granny Dera's....46

Salads
Beth's Cornbread Salad....37
Green Bean Salad....38
Orange Fluff Salad....36
Scrumptious Layered Salad....36
Suzanne's Broccoli Salad....37

Side Dishes and Vegetables
Arkansas Green Beans....88
Aunt Janice's Bean Pot....92
Brown Sugar Carrots....86
Consommé Rice....85
Fried Apples....85

Gerald's Fresh Corn on the Cob....89
Happy New Year Black-Eyed Peas....84
Luke's Okra....87
Macaroni and Cheese....90
Morgan's Green Bean Bundle....87
Ms. Vera's Cheesy Corn Casserole....89
Parmesan Roasted Green Beans....88
Peggy's Broccoli Casserole....85
Poke Salat....77
POTATOES
Cheesy Hash Brown Casserole....93
Our Favorite Mashed Potatoes....137
Potato Pancakes....86
RiverWood's Bacon Hash Brown Casserole....93
Rosemary Roasted Sweet Potatoes....88
Skillet Candied Sweet Potatoes....87
Skillet Roasted Corn and Black Bean Salsa....84
Sweet Potato Pie, Granny Dera's....46
Sautéed Cabbage....90
Tomato Grits....91
Turnip Greens, Gerald's....80

Soups

Moma Holt's Potato Soup....39
Shrimp and Bean Soup....39
Spicy Chicken-Tomato Pantry Soup....40
Venison Stew with Veggies....40

This & That

Fresh Blueberry Syrup....23
Frosty Homemade Ice Cream....23
Homemade Whipped Cream....22
Merry Christmas French Toast....22
Snow Cream....102

Recipe Contributors

The following recipes were graciously contributed by Alabama cooks who shared their treasured family recipes.

J.D. Dillard
Our Favorite Mashed Potatoes....137
Jo Anne Dillard
Ma-Maw McKee's Chocolate Cake....110
Ms. Charlcey's Best Sweet Potato Pie....117
German Chocolate Upside-Down Cake....111
Leah Dillard
Our Favorite Pumpkin Pie....136
Lonna Dillard
Apple Cake....111
No Bake Chocolate Oatmeal Cookies....128
Wyatt Dillard
Our Favorite Mashed Potatoes....137
Dinah Douglas
Mountain Dew Dumplings....126
Dinah's Stuffed Jalapeno Peppers....20
Cheesy Hash Brown Casserole....93
Linda Parker Gorum
Hamburger Bean Casserole....64
Betty Lewis
Betty's Shrimp Chowder....72
Rosemary Roasted Sweet Potatoes....88
Stuffed Bell Peppers....63
Strawberry Layer Cake....112
Shrimp and Bean Soup....39
Lillian Sanders Parker
Applesauce Raisin Muffins....129
Pork Chop Skillet Dinner....67
Chicken Casserole....54
Lillian's Coconut Cream Pies....120
Green Bean Salad....38
Kim Scott
Kim's Sausage Roll....58
Kim's Mexican Cornbread....14
Sue Parker Shipp
Butter Roll Dessert....43
Syrup Cake....44
Tomato Grits....91
Apple Sauce Cake....115
Cheddar Cheese and Chicken Casserole....53
Charles and Phyllis Shirley
Peggy's Broccoli Casserole....85
Aunt Virgie Holt's Chili Sauce....20
Southern Punchbowl Cake....109
Granny's Divinity....129
David Standridge
David's Oven Fried Fish....72

Dera Standridge
Skillet Candied Sweet Potatoes 87
Old-Fashioned Banana Pudding....124
Granny Dera's Old Fashioned Chocolate Pie.....118
Granny's Egg Custard....126
Old Fashioned Coconut Pies 121
Jasper Standridge
Our Favorite Cornbread 136
Morgan Standridge
Consommé Rice 85
Morgan's Green Bean Bundles....87
Pat Standridge
Poppy Seed Bread....15
Mocha Punch 21
Cherry Dump Cake 106
Mom's Comfort Chicken 53
Sydney Standridge
Our Favorite Scrambled Eggs....117
Donna Statham
Macaroni and Cheese 98
Donna's Pecan Pie Muffins 130
Pimento Cheese 20
Lemon Crescent Rolls....131
Pecan Tassies 131
Cousin Donna's Italian Cream Cake....113
Hummingbird Cake 116
Cindy Swann
Broccoli and Chicken Casserole 54
Gerald Swann
Gerald's Cornbread 80
Gerald's Turnip Greens 80
Gerald's Fresh Corn on the Cob....89
Glenda Swann
Glenda Swann's Red Velvet Cake 108
Lorene Swann
Lorene's Skillet-Fried Chicken 52
Lorene's One Pot Meal 68
Shirley Swann
Shirley Swann's Spiced Tea....21
Gran-Gran's Hot Tamales....59
Fried Apples 85
Sunday Best Pot Roast 62
Granny Campbell's Chocolate Pudding 123
Potato Pancakes....86
Venison Roast 70
Shirley's Saucy Pork Chops 67
Aunt Janice's Bean Pot....92
Beth Thigpen
Beth and Phil's Shrimp Gumbo....71
Beth's Cornbread Salad....37
Suzanne Wood
RiverWood's Bacon Hash Brown Casserole.........93
Fabulous RiverWood Venison Tenderloin with Mushroom Cream Sauce....69
Brown Sugar Carrots 86
Luke's Okra....87
Arkansas Green Beans 88
Suzanne's Broccoli Salad....37
Parmesan Roasted Green Beans....88

Weights and Measures

dash = less than 1/8 teaspoon
3 teaspoons = 1 tablespoon (T)
2 tablespoons = 1 liquid ounce
4 tablespoons = 1/4 cup (C)
5 1/2 tablespoons = 1/3 cup
8 tablespoons = 1/2 cup
16 tablespoons = 1 cup
2 cups = 1 pint
2 pints = 1 quart
4 quarts = 1 gallon
16 ounces = 1 pound
2 cups, liquid = 1 pound
2 cups butter = 1 pound
2 cups granulated sugar = 1 pound
4 cups flour = 1 pound
chocolate, 1 square bitter = 1 ounce
3 T cocoa + 1 T fat (butter) = 1 ounce chocolate
cheese, 4 cups grated = 1 pound
8 egg whites = 1 cup approx.
16 egg yolks = 1 cup approx.
lemon, juice of 1 = 2 to 3 tablespoons
macaroni, 1 cup raw = 2 cups cooked
rice, 1 cup raw = 3 to 4 cups cooked
rice, 1 lb. raw = 2 cups
chicken fryer, cooked = 3 cups chopped
1 T cornstarch = 2 T flour for thickener

Oven Temperatures
250-300 = slow
325 = slow–moderate
350 = moderate
375 = quick–moderate
400 = moderately hot
425-450 = hot
475-500 = very hot

Proportions
1 cup rice:2 cups water
1 cup grits:4 cups water

Sauces/Gravy
Thin 2T flour:1 cup liquid:2T fat
Medium 3T flour:1 cup liquid:3T fat
Heavy 1/3 c flour:1 cup liquid:3T fat